The Living Memories Project

The Living Memories Project

Legacies That Last

by

Meryl Ain

Arthur M. Fischman

Stewart Ain

LITTLE MIAMI PUBLISHING CO.
Milford, Ohio
2014

Little Miami Publishing Co.
P.O. Box 588
Milford, Ohio 45150-0588
http://www.littlemiamibooks.com

First Edition

ISBN-13: 978-0-9882553-7-1

Library of Congress Catalog Card Number: 2013957332

Printed in Canada.

Dedication

*In Living and Loving Memory of
Our Mother, Mother-in-Law, and Muse,
Helen Trachtenberg Fischman.
Our Motivation and Inspiration for the
Living Memories Project
May Her Memory Always be for a Blessing.*

> "*There are stars whose light reaches the earth only after they themselves have disintegrated. And there are individuals whose memory lights the world after they have passed from it. These lights shine even in the darkest night and illumine our path . . .*"
>
> — Hannah Senesh —

Contents

Acknowledgments

We THANK ALL OF THOSE WHO GENEROUSLY shared with us their inspiring accounts of how they have carried on the memories of their loved ones. We truly appreciate their honesty, openness, insights, and time; their stories both motivated and comforted us, and we hope they will do the same for our readers.

We also thank the many people who sent us background information, photographs, and other source materials that were so important in helping us bring to life these wonderful stories.

Thank you as well to all of our friends and family who thought this book was a good idea, encouraged us, and believed in us and this project. We are grateful for their sustained interest and the countless leads and suggestions they offered.

Our boundless love for our children gives meaning and focus to our lives and our work. Their overall support and enthusiasm for our efforts were a driving force in seeing this project to fruition. We especially thank Rabbi Dan Ain for his spiritual insights; Jonathan Ain and Halie Geller for their legal perspective; Michael "Morty" Ain, Molly Fischman, Beth Ain, and Alana Joblin Ain for their literary and linguistic sensitivities and ideas. Special thanks to Anna Fischman for her photographic expertise and for kindly spending many hours assisting with the book's pictures.

Thanks also to Janet Margolies for her creative ideas, thoughtful critique, and unflagging support, all of which helped us to shape and develop our goals for this project. Special thanks to Roberta Ain for her ongoing encouragement and wholehearted interest.

Finally, this book would never have come to light without a publisher, and we thank Howard Ain for introducing us to Barbara Gargiulo of Little Miami Publishing Company. Barbara immediately "got it" and we are truly grateful to her for lovingly shepherding the birth of *The Living Memories Project*.

Introductions

Learning to Remember
by Meryl Ain and Arthur Fischman

Ask anyone the question, "Who has had the most significant impact on your life?" and you're likely to hear about a parent or grandparent, a sibling, a teacher, a neighbor, or a friend. The impact may be direct, such as the lessons or behavioral model offered by a parent, or it may be more subtle yet no less significant—perhaps the spawning by a teacher or friend of an interest that later developed into a full-blown talent or skill.

True story: Before either of us was old enough to read or write, we could name all the U.S. presidents (in order), all the U.S. state capitals and most of the world capitals, and even recite Edgar Allan Poe's "The Raven" from memory. In teaching us—and drilling us on—all of these names, places, and words, our grandfather hoped to prepare us for a future appearance on one of those new "big-money" quiz shows so popular in the 1950s. Although we still haven't made it on to a game show, our grandfather's attention and persistence were responsible for our learning *how* to learn—a skill that has made it easy for both of us, to this day, to absorb and retain large amounts of information, even in subject areas in which we have no background or formal training. And every time we sit around a table with relatives and remember some long-lost bit of family lore that no one else recalls, we pay fond tribute to the man who spent his last years teaching us how to remember.

Our grandfather's influence has lived on long after his death. The people whom we interviewed for this book tell similar stories, as do many of the most public figures of our day, whose experiences in this area are often front-page news. For some, a symbol celebrates what a departed individual stood for. Prince William, for example, remembered his late mother, Princess Diana, when he presented his fiancée, Kate Middleton, with her sapphire and diamond engagement ring. He said, "It was my way of making sure my mother didn't miss out on today and the excitement." He added, "It's very special to me. As Kate's very special to me now, it was right to put the two together."

For others, someone's words or actions were the catalyst for an artistic endeavor or even an entire career. After Paul McCartney's late mother came to him in a dream during a difficult period in his life and told him to "let it be," he wrote a song with that title as a way to show his gratitude for her "visit" and to share her advice with the world.

Or Susan Boyle. Encouraged by her mother to become a contestant on *Britain's Got Talent*, she entered the competition after her mother's death. Although she believed she was too old to compete and had never sung in front of an audience anywhere near as large as this one, she saw her appearance as the first step toward carving out a singing career for herself and thereby paying tribute to her mother. She was runner-up and, from her very first appearance, a worldwide media sensation.

A survivor who lost both parents and a sister during the Holocaust, Elie Wiesel set down his experiences in Auschwitz and Buchenwald in *La Nuit* (Night), a memoir that has brought a firsthand perspective on the horrors of the death camps to millions of people around the world. After being unable, for a decade, to write or speak about what he had seen and endured, he finally put his thoughts and memories on paper "to testify, to stop the dead from dying." Wiesel received the Nobel Peace Prize and the Congressional Medal of Freedom, among other awards.

Having received encouragement and support from his father to become a performer, Billy Crystal became a highly successful standup comedian and actor. He paid homage to his father by writing and performing the Tony Award–winning *700 Sundays*, a one-person play whose title reflects the time the two had together before his father's death, which occurred when Crystal was fourteen.

Still others who suffered the loss of a spouse or child or sibling may have found in the personality of that loved one a reason to go on, and perhaps in the death itself a cause worth bringing to life. After the kidnapping and murder of his six-year-old son, John Walsh ended his career as a successful businessman and launched a campaign to protect children and bring to justice those who would harm them. He became host of *America's Most Wanted*, a television show that has assisted law enforcement in apprehending more than a thousand dangerous criminals and recovering dozens of missing children. He and his wife established the Adam Walsh Child Resource Center and have been the driving force behind major child protection legislation.

A promise made in response to a request from her dying sister led Nancy Brinker to establish Susan G. Komen for the Cure, an organization that has raised more than one billion dollars since 1980 in support of breast cancer research, education, and community healthcare. The annual "Race for the Cure" attracts more than one million participants throughout the United States and internationally. In 2008, Brinker was included on *Time* magazine's list of the one hundred most influential people in the world.

Rep. Carolyn McCarthy ran for Congress as a gun-control advocate following the murder of her husband and the wounding of her son by a crazed gunman on the Long Island Railroad. She has introduced several important pieces of legislation designed to increase firearms safety and place greater restrictions on ownership of assault weapons.

The idea of keeping alive those who remain important to us even in death is firmly rooted in various cultures. *El Dia de los Muertos* (the Day of the Dead), for example, is a centuries-old annual celebration in which many Latin Americans remember departed loved ones with rituals that include the building of altars and decoration of graves. Through the ages, other cultures—including those in Egypt and Indonesia—have observed their own rituals to honor the dead.

After our mother's death in November 2006, we felt a void in our lives. Yes, she was eighty-five and had enjoyed, by any measure, a long, full life, but this was someone who, until her final illness, took no medicine and looked at least ten years younger than her age. She was the picture of health, right up to the end. Her mind was still sharp, her sense of humor intact, and, were it not for the freak cancer that invaded her body, we

Helen and Herbert Fischman Wedding.

had no doubt that she would have made it to one hundred.

It was clear to us that our mother would always remain in our lives and that continued efforts to achieve what is commonly referred to as "closure" would be futile. The only path that made sense to us was to accept and embrace our mother's continued presence and somehow turn it into something tangible, as it had been for us during her lifetime.

Inspired by so many others who had paid tribute in some meaningful way to a deceased loved one, we wondered how we could integrate our mother's spirit and values into our lives—not just once, but every day. We heard or read about and, in some cases, witnessed first-hand the high-profile tributes undertaken to honor the memory of a loved one. In conducting our research for the book, we also learned about quieter, more private and personal ways of keeping alive the lessons and the values of those who played such a huge role in helping to shape us into the people we now are. Family recipes, poems, a favorite song or even a favorite color—all have been used to invoke the presence of a loved one and to pass down to the next generation a sense of what made this person so special.

But what about closure—that word we mentioned a few paragraphs ago? Isn't this kind of living tribute pretty much the exact opposite of closure? Doesn't there come a time when we just need to move on with our lives and leave the past in the past? Syndicated radio host Dr. Dan Gottlieb, a Philadelphia-based family therapist, dismisses the whole notion of closure. "I think it is a misconception or misinterpretation of Elisabeth Kubler-Ross," he says. "It's not what she meant. You have issues in your life. You have memories. You have longings and aches. Nothing goes away."

This book began as a way for the authors to deal with their own longings and aches in a constructive way. And perhaps there could be no more appropriate tribute to our mother than writing a book. She was, after all, a lover of words and someone who did a lot of writing herself. A proud graduate of NYU, she joined the Women's Army Corps shortly after receiving her diploma and went to work as editor of the *Fort Belvoir* (Virginia)

Helen Fischman during WWII.

Castle, where she remained until the end of World War II. As young children, we remember our mother sitting at the kitchen table, night after night, the tap-tap-tap of the typewriter keys going on long past our bedtime as she attempted to reduce her many recollections of military life to a marketable manuscript. She never did get that manuscript published, but that didn't stop her years later, at almost eighty years of age, from writing a longer memoir that covered much more ground. "A Woman of the 20th Century," which begins with her grandparents' courtship in a small town in Austria and goes on to recount her many adventures as manager of patient accounts at a large hospital, was never published either. But getting published was not uppermost in her mind when she sat down to put her life on paper. What she wanted more than anything was to leave behind, for her children and grandchildren, information about their roots—the answers to questions likely to be asked long after she was no longer there to answer them. In providing those answers, she also left us the description of a remarkable life.

Just as we hoped to honor our mother's essential goodness, cheerfulness, and optimism by writing this book, we hope that every reader can find comfort and meaning through honoring the memory and values, and the positive, never-ending influence, of one no longer here.

Putting Memories in Focus
by Stewart Ain

MEMORIES—FROM THE TIME WE WERE KIDS my identical twin brother, Howard, and I unwittingly began to preserve family memories. We received our first reel-to-reel tape recorder when we were twelve, and as the embryonic journalists we were, we began interviewing and recording our family members. As youngsters, we certainly didn't realize the impact of what we were doing. But now, more than fifty years later, the family tapestry of what we recorded is priceless.

Our two grandfathers were both self-made men who fulfilled the American Dream. Our paternal grandfather bought and sold candy stores in various locations, always near a subway. My favorite story that he shared with us was of the candy store across the street from Yankee Stadium; his customers included the Yankee ballplayers, most notably Babe Ruth and Lou Gehrig. Gehrig regularly came to buy a pack of Camel cigarettes. My other grandfather, who also came to this country as a penniless immigrant, established a lighting fixture business, which required him to travel all over the world. We recorded his many exploits, and can still relive them.

Our two grandmothers gave us the family history and recounted the experiences we shared with them, such as the times our grandmother Etta took us to rock 'n' roll concerts. Our parents weren't fans—but our swinging grandma shared our love for our generation's music.

We also recorded important family events, such as our sister Roberta's bat mitzvah rehearsals. Every year the entire extended family—aunts, uncles, cousins, etc.—went to Colonial Terrace in Peekskill, New York, for Thanksgiving. Howard and I interviewed them all.

It wasn't until our grandparents died that I began to realize the value of our "hobby."

A generation later we switched to videotape, and as our own children grew, the videos became all the more precious. When my wife, Meryl, lost her father in 2005 after a ten-year decline in his health, watching him alive and happy in the videos provided some comfort.

But a year and a half later, when Meryl's mother died suddenly after a brief illness, we were devastated. My mother-in-law was a gracious, generous, and intelligent person, who volunteered to sew on my buttons (no reflection on my wife), and kept copies of all my *New York Times* stories before they became accessible online. She delighted in baking my favorite desserts—brownies and apple pie—whenever we went to her house or when she came to ours. She gave me so much loving attention that I often teased Meryl that she loved me more than her daughter.

Of course, that wasn't true. Meryl and her mother had an amazing relationship, and when she died, Meryl was bereft. But she had learned from her mother to be proactive. She told me that her mother always had advised her that when she was sad, bored, or depressed to "get a project." A project could be anything from cleaning out a closet to writing a book. So Meryl convinced her brother, Arthur, and me to join her in writing *The Living Memories Project*.

We interviewed the people who graciously consented to share their narratives with us for the book. As a journalist, I was interested in and impressed by their stories. Their courage and creativity were inspiring. While we were working on the book, my mother became gravely ill and died seven months later. That is when the project really began to hit home for me.

How could I preserve the positive memories of my mother, when what was fresh in my mind was the incredible suffering she endured? I will always remember how she fought the cancer until the last day of her life. She so wanted to stay alive for my father, who had Alzheimer's and died five months later.

As I reflect on our book, I know that all three of us have been helped in working through our own grief by the inspiration of those who generously shared their stories. I hope that, like many of the individuals in our book, I will be able to preserve positive memories of my parents and let go of any negative ones associated with their illnesses. The book has been a source of guidance as I grapple with the most meaningful way to carry on my parents' memory. I want to remember them embracing life and counting their many blessings. It is my hope that our readers will also find a way to preserve the memories of their loved ones in a way that is significant and comforting to them.

Stewart, Howard, and Roberta with mother and grandparents.

CHAPTER 1

Death is not Fatal

— as shared by Malachy McCourt

Malachy McCourt is a writer, actor, and raconteur. Born in Brooklyn, he was raised in Limerick, Ireland, from the age of three and lost three siblings by the time he was five years old. He left school at thirteen to work as a laborer and, at twenty, returned to the United States, where he worked as a longshoreman, truck loader, and dishwasher before becoming an actor. He has appeared in numerous movies and television soap operas and worked as a New York radio talk show host in the 1970s. He also opened a bar in Manhattan—Malachy's—which became famous for its celebrity clientele and was, according to some, the original singles' bar. McCourt has written several books, including two memoirs—A Monk Swimming *and* Singing My Him Song. *He coauthored and starred in the play* A Couple of Blaguards *with his brother Frank (the author of* Angela's Ashes*), who died in July 2009.*

ଐ

WE HAVE AN ATTITUDE ABOUT DEATH IN IRELAND. It's not, as I often say, fatal because we keep people alive so much in song and in story. I suppose I'm reluctant to let people go and so therefore have constructed a spirit that stays around to enjoy whatever has to be

McCourt family montage.
[WITH PERMISSION OF MALACHY MCCOURT.]

enjoyed but is freed from the troubles of the world. So you keep them alive by entertaining them—and them entertaining us—by reliving their lives, singing songs, talking about their eccentricities, and therefore they don't die.

A month after you die, you have a Catholic Mass and you're supposed to send the soul on its way. That is a relic of an old pagan custom. But the Irish don't let the soul go—they say the soul is in heaven, but it is a heaven that's on Earth and that sticks with you. That is the memory and they say someone is watching you and that she or he is in a better place—free of troubles and free to enjoy the good things of the afterlife without having to deal with life in Ireland and famine and war and horrible depression.

I think of the afterlife as a very large pizza pie and we all become part of the ingredients and make it bigger as we die. Five billion dead and six billion alive and so eleven billion have been born, which does away with reincarnation because with five billion dead we can only have ten billion born. Do we keep getting reincarnated? I don't know and I don't care. Like everyone, I wonder what happens. A few weeks ago I sat there watching Frank die. He was in a coma for the last couple of days of his life and I, figuring that nobody is really in a coma and he could still hear what I was saying almost in a stream of consciousness, sang songs and recited poetry. He didn't respond in any way, and then, on a Sunday afternoon at 3:02—people say we draw our last breath, but no, we expel it—he was breathing very lightly and all of a sudden it was gone and there was no movement and it was amazing how fast it happened. I had been holding his hand and how fast the body gets cold when the heart stops beating. The blood begins to cool.

I don't think I'm spiritual about it. Cessation is what I felt. This body has stopped working. I thought about it but I'm thinking now that whatever spirituality I may have felt was just my invoking what I've read and my indoctrination by the clergy, who make you keep your faith by fear: If I don't have faith, I have to fear hell. It is not my choice to think of death with anger. It is simply a nice way of taking another journey. I don't know where.

I was around five when the twins died and I find Oliver dead beside me in the bed. It was very mysterious—the dying of them. They put them in boxes and into the ground and they are in heaven and you accept that as a kid. Eleven classmates died between the ages of six and eleven; that was how you got used to death. When Paddy O'Brien got fast-killing TB in the summer, we worried that he might die while on holiday and we wouldn't get a half day off from school for the funeral. We sent Frank over to say think about us, and Frank said if you die before the summer is out I'll kill you.

People always say never speak ill of the dead, but I figure it's the only time you can because they can't get back at you. And so, with keeping people alive, we only think about them in sayings and poetry and music and keeping alive whatever talents they had, but we need to keep the evil ones alive, too. We can't allow Hitler to die or we'll forget what he did. So malevolence and evil and anger must also be used to keep people alive. People need to be remembered for that.

I don't have to do anything consciously to keep Frank alive. I think of him every day. Before *Ashes*, I spoke with him every day and we performed a play, convulsed with laughter. The script was merely the program and off we'd go on the program. My mother came to see it one time and she was outraged by the bawdiness of it. Frank and I were going to do our show in Pottstown, Pennsylvania, and we were driving there on Saint Patrick's Day, long before *Angela's Ashes*. It was a sunny day and we got on 380 in Pennsylvania and it became dark and threatening and we went into a sleet storm and it was like going through a curtain into another world and freezing. I didn't know the road was so slick and I was going sixty-five when a big truck loomed up ahead and it was like the side of the Titanic. I put my foot down on the brake to slow down and nothing happened. We went forward at sixty-five and I shouted to Frank to hold on and he, with supreme irony, calmly said, "To what?" And I always remember that.

In the depths of whatever grief we have, there is always something about the people we love who have died that has offended us, annoyed us, or made us uncomfortable. It's okay to remember them and forgive if you want, but you don't have to. Resentment is like taking poison and waiting for the other person to die. Don't let it consume you. Once you accept that a person is dead, let it go. With someone you love, you don't have to keep the bad going but accept that you're feeling that. Jews have the monopoly on guilt, Catholics on remorse, and the Irish let everything go. So the main thing is, don't feel guilty about anything. There is no way you can make amends to the dead. Let it go. Just don't do it again. The way I look at things now is, I can do nothing about those who are dead. I'm adhering to Oscar Wilde's maxim: *Forgive your enemies. It annoys them.* That is what I'm doing. I'm enjoying my life and will be seventy-eight on Sunday and live every day as if it is my last.

CHAPTER 2

Music and Social Justice

— as shared by Jen Chapin

Singer/songwriter Jen Chapin is the daughter of the late folk rock icon Harry Chapin, who was killed in a car accident on the Long Island Expressway in 1981 at the age of thirty-eight. Eight years after that tragedy, the eighteen-year-old Chapin began attending Brown University, where, after studying in Zimbabwe and Mexico, she received a degree in international relations. She later studied at Berklee College of Music and began a career in music. She has been critically acclaimed as an urban folk singer and her recordings hailed as, among other things, "soulfully poetic," politically aware," and "brilliant." She is married to jazz bassist

Jen Chapin
[PHOTO BY MERRI CYR.]

Stephan Crump, with whom she often performs. The couple lives in Brooklyn with their two children.

Jen Chapin (www.jenchapin.com) has devoted much of her time, including two terms as chair of the board of directors, to WhyHunger (formerly known as World Hunger Year), an organization cofounded by her father in 1975 in the hopes of combating hunger and poverty through grassroots action. Members of the Chapin family—including Jen's siblings, uncles and cousins—as well as friends of the family, frequently perform concerts to pay tribute to Harry Chapin and to raise money for WhyHunger.

⁖

My DAD WAS A REAL FAMILY MAN, especially just in keeping the extended family together by virtue of his enthusiasm. He brought his brothers together musically and asked them to work with him. He was friendly and outgoing and was a real force in my extended family. This concert and his music continue to bring us together in ways that we wouldn't normally be. We're onstage and collaborating and having a musical relationship. I do four songs—two in the first half and two in second. And then I just hang out backstage with my cousins and uncles and former members of my dad's band. It's meaningful and relaxing. There is nothing like down time. I'm getting paid for it and don't feel guilty about it. I just get to hang out with my cousins and play with each other's kids and exchange family gossip. It brings people together and that's my favorite part—just hanging out—and my relationship with everybody.

Tom's wife, Aunt Bonnie, will often be there even though she doesn't perform. Tom's daughters didn't know Harry. Abigail was born two years before he died and Lily two weeks before he died. But now they will have a relationship with Uncle Harry because of the music.

Sixty to 70 percent of the music we play in the show is Harry's music. I do 50 percent of my own. My two uncles will do some of their songs and they also have to cover some of the hits. My uncle will

Jen Chapin with dad, Harry Chapin..
[PHOTO BY TOM CHAPIN.]

do one of my grandfather's songs and songs from the era, but not necessarily my dad's songs.

My decision on what I play is a musical decision. My dad's songs are meaningful. They are my dad's songs and so they say something by virtue of their existence. I have to feel I can render them in an effective way.

I was a shy little kid and I can look at the life I have chosen now and the fact I love the unexpected in my schedule. I like improvisation in day-to-day life. I'm not a nine-to-five person and things were always a little crazy. There was always a lot of stuff going on, a lot of people coming in and out. There were always new people. My house was open to sometimes-eccentric characters—not typical, and very enriching. My parents weren't very discriminating and people would come in who had questionable hygiene or talked too loud. My mother always said that when she married my father she thought he had everything in the family—black, gay, people who had handicaps, and just weird. She figured raising kids in this family would mean they would be tolerant—and that was attractive to her. Just the fact he was a musician made it a more supportive environment. His performance style was honest and real. I like spectacle, but that was never my choice, and I suppose that came from him. He was a reference point. I saw him perform many times. He wanted to bring us along and not separate that part of our lives, and whenever he could convince my mother to take us out of school we went along.

There is a song of his—"Jenny"—and he told a story about it onstage. He said he was stuck for a lyric and he looked down and saw me drawing a picture that I had titled *Rainbow of Love*. And he put that in the song. I don't think it is one of his finest lyrics—it was just what I was drawing as an eight-year-old.

I don't really have a favorite song of his. But "Cat's in the Cradle" is just an amazing, bulletproof piece of craft that will not go away as far as resonance . . . and my mother wrote the lyrics. "Shooting Star" is dramatic in its performance and it's something I love to sing. And, in the Chapin Family shows, I often do "Tangled Up Puppet."

Paying tribute to my dad with programs for the needy wasn't a decision we made—it was obvious. That is what he did. We never looked at it in those terms—let's help the less fortunate. It is about America and social justice and stopping from living the lie of saying this is the American dream when now one-quarter of our kids are hungry. The decision was made by the world and not in a family meeting. It was just the reality of the values we were raised with and how we could have meaningful lives. We were interested in being a part of the communities in which we lived and not just paying property taxes. My father said hunger was an obscenity and that hunger in America is the ultimate obscenity. And my mother was a silent partner in this. There shouldn't be hunger in the world. Humanity is well beyond the capacity to not have hunger; there is no need for it. We never accepted it.

My dad felt compassionately about democracy and one of his mentors was Frances Moore Lappé, who said hunger is not from a scarcity of food but a scarcity of democracy. The premise is that we have the ability to feed ourselves many times over. We can't stand to have hunger on Long Island—which comprises two of the wealthiest counties—and internationally it is not acceptable. So when he died there was no question but that we would try to continue his work. We all chose different paths, and by the time he passed on it was just part of who we were.

I am now secretary of the board of directors of WhyHunger. That has been my main involvement. And I pitch in when called upon by Long Island Cares. I feel a direct connection to my dad through that work. Long Island Cares does direct aid. WhyHunger asks questions and tries to do systemic reform to get food around the world safely and securely. We really believe—and so did my dad—that problems exist in local communities. From community gardens to job training programs, low-income housing and financial literacy programs, there is an amazing spectrum of solutions and WhyHunger works to network and support those solutions.

It's not like all my activism is public. I do a lot of writing and stuffing envelopes and that kind of thing—volunteering. That is such a significant part of my life and how I spend my day. The music is also private and public.

I don't really go to his gravesite. I don't have conversations with him as people often do with loved ones who have passed. I don't have the need. I have so many ways of communing with him and I know he is proud of me and I have an ongoing dialogue with him and read his speeches about social justice and they are so much today—what he wrote about and sang about—they are so current and I feel so connected. I have ongoing dialogue through my own work. So in a way I am privileged he was a public person and, almost every time I perform, someone comes up and speaks of him and remembers him. Other people passed on in my life and it's a sad thing that the person is not here and that I have to keep him alive. But with dad, I don't have that because he is everywhere in my life and so many people's lives—thousands I met and that I will never meet.

Psychiatrists have found in studies that people are most fulfilled when they are involved in a cause greater than themselves or through school or block associations or local soup kitchens. One of the largest arguments for being involved is selfishness. It makes you happier. That applies to people in mourning and not in mourning.

After September 11 there were people who built schools in Afghanistan. They have peace, as opposed to those who want to punish the villain and who live lonelier, sadder lives. Carolyn McCarthy, after her son was injured and her husband killed by a gunman on the Long Island Rail Road, ran for Congress. There are so many different things you can do instead of just closing up shop. She has a new identity.

My advice is the same for those who have lost as it is for those who haven't: Whether your father is a talented artist or not and whether you have career aspirations or not, write a song or do some other satisfying endeavor. It's good for the soul.

CHAPTER 3

Constructive Revenge

— as shared by Robert Meeropol

Robert Meeropol
[WITH PERMISSION OF ROBERT MEEROPOL.]

*R*obert Meeropol's parents, Julius and Ethel Rosenberg, were executed on June 19, 1953, for conspiracy to commit espionage against the United States. Meeropol was six—his brother, Michael, was ten. The boys had a difficult childhood, being moved from one temporary living situation to another until they were adopted by Abel and Anne Meeropol. Over the course of thirty years, Robert studied anthropology (almost earning a doctorate in the field), "dabbled" in teaching, and worked as a lawyer, but nowhere did he find the inner satisfaction he craved. As he became increasingly unhappy in his law practice, Meeropol *felt intense pressure to do something different—"something that would transform the negatives of childhood into something positive."*

The epiphany came in December 1988, after he met Patricia Gros Levasseur, who, along with her husband and another defendant, had been convicted at the "Ohio 7" trial and were now being tried for sedition as well. For the trio's involvement with a radical left-wing organization, this thirty-four-year-old mother of three young daughters faced decades in prison if convicted in the second trial. Meeropol, who could relate immediately to what the Levasseur children were

Ethel and Julius Rosenberg in the park, circa 1942.
[WITH PERMISSION OF ROBERT MEEROPOL.]

going through, started the *Rosenberg Fund for Children (www.rfc.org)* to benefit the children of targeted prisoners.

℀

I HAVE NO DETAILED MEMORY of my and my brother's prison visits to our parents, nor do I have any recollection at all of our final visit to them at Sing Sing Correctional Facility in Ossining, New York, shortly before their execution. What I do remember of our visits is that we played games and saw them one at a time. They were very calm during the visits—except for the last one where my brother got upset. They wanted to create for us a sense of a normal family—of normalcy—as much as they could, and that dovetailed with what I wanted. It was a very upsetting time and a sense of danger was in the air. I didn't know where it was coming from, but I knew bad forces were out there and I had to be quiet or they would get us. That sense of anxiety hovered about and I wanted calm, so the best thing to do was to be calm. The adults were calm and I had that desire for calm and normalcy. My parents were trying to do that and so it meshed together perfectly.

As I grew up, one thought became central to my philosophy—the concept of constructive revenge. The good thing about revenge is that it's active; the bad thing is that it's destructive action. Others respond to misfortune by becoming passive; they just mourn and die a little themselves or become negative and cynical and self-destructive. All of those things are negative. The idea of constructive revenge is to take that energy and channel it into a positive direction. If you succeed, it is better for society, and you feel better because you get external positive reaction and internal satisfaction.

I encountered this on a personal level when I got involved in anti-capital-punishment work. When I met Renny Cushing, he was head of Murder Victims' Families for Reconciliation, an organization for folks who believe that capital punishment is a human rights violation, even after an immediate family member has been murdered or executed or has disappeared. (He is now head of Murder Victims' Families for Human Rights.) His father was murdered and he decided to found the organization, and is crusading now for this cause, in honor of his father. Once again, a positive response, and that is why I say it has permeated my entire philosophy. Look at capital punishment—someone is killed and so we kill the murderer. That's a negative response to a negative and the only way to stop it is with a positive response.

There was a pressure valve I was searching for and it also was an event that triggered it. I was in law practice for several years and becoming more and more unhappy when I met a woman who was a defendant in a major political trial—the Ohio 7 case. She was only charged with harboring a fugitive—her husband—but she was being tried again and facing sixty years in prison. She told me that the children of two of her codefendants—who were aged eleven, eight, and five—were seized and interrogated without their parents. That never happened to me and I was thinking that I didn't even know about this. This happened in December and I left the law firm at the end of January. In April 1989, at four in the morning, I woke up and sat up in bed. I always had this dream of starting a foundation in my parents' name but I never knew what it would do. Now I knew—it would be for kids of targeted prisoners. It took until September 1990 to get it off the ground, and I broadened the concept to include political prisoners and targeted activists. It was because of that incident—the combination of finding out the stories of these children while I was desperately looking to do something.

In establishing the Rosenberg Fund for Children, I found more than constructive revenge—it's really a positive response that is the most satisfying. I decided to name the organization after my parents so they would be associated with a fund that helps children, rather than be remembered as two people executed as spies by the United States.

We select people who have gotten into trouble while engaged in trying to transform society. They are not pure. We may disagree with what they are doing, but we look at their motivations and try to make something positive out of it. We celebrate the parents' resistance by benefiting their children. In doing so, I'm able to celebrate my parents' resistance, rather than mourning their fate.

The first impulse is to give the most dramatic example of how we help children, such as the story of someone who is traumatized and needs intensive therapy. But other times I find myself telling the story of someone who goes out and participates in a demonstration, the boss finds out and the person is fired. For a single parent this is a serious thing, and if the child is a talented musician there is no money for music lessons. So the fund steps in and provides money for the music lesson and that music lesson can be like a safe port in a storm, and that's the way I think.

Although I'm in my early sixties and as old as the grandparents of the children we're helping, I still look at these tragic situations from a child's perspective, which is why I believe this work has been success-ful. I have no way of really knowing what my parents would think of the fund, but ultimately I don't care. It is what works for me. I see it as a positive thing.

It took me till forty-three and this tragedy happened to me between the ages of three and six, so it was a very long and slow pro-cess. But when I look back, sometimes I feel that every choice I made was getting me closer to a subconscious goal. When I look at the fund, I think it's really good I worked as a lawyer and at a magazine and worked for the reopening effort and did lobbying and fundraising and went to grad school—all of them were elements I took with me when I finally figured it out. So even if you don't like what you're doing, there are probably positive things to take from it. I didn't figure out a lot of them while they were happening, but if you try to take some-thing positive from them, you will and it will be very satisfying.

CHAPTER 4

The Comfort of Memory Quilts

— as shared by Eileen Belmont

Eileen Belmont is a Philadelphia quilt artist who creates memory quilts for people wishing to remember and pay tribute to departed loved ones in a heartfelt way. Belmont has been sewing since she was eleven, having learned the skill from her mother, a science and home economics teacher. When she began sewing under the label "ei of the needle" more than thirty years ago, Belmont was making home décor items as well as clothing for herself and her three daughters. Along the way she started making quilts and, in 2007, left the security of her full-time employment to focus her creative energy on quilt-

Eileen Belmont with her mother.

ing. Today she designs and constructs art quilts, wall hangings, lap quilts, and bed quilts for her many clients. She realized that people have an attachment to their favorite clothing. By combining this realization with her skillful quilting artistry, she channeled "ei of the needle" into a vehicle for helping people save their memories.

৵

My FIRST FOCUS WAS MAKING DECORATIVE PILLOWS using T-shirts. People often design T-shirts to commemorate an event and often buy them to remember a favorite vacation. I started using them along with other textiles to make collections of pillows from colleges or from favorite sports teams. Sometimes I would instead use novelty fabric—ballet fabric for a dancer, or musical-notes fabric for a kid involved in theater—and then my business evolved into making a quilt or making a wall hanging using more than one textile. People would add their own mementos, such as a label from a Phillies cap or the insignia from a tote bag or a tassel from graduation.

Memory quilts are celebration quilts. They're a way to celebrate memories of all kinds—the memory of someone who has passed away, the memory of a lifecycle event. Some of my commissions celebrate people who are living. Others are to memorialize someone who has passed, and so the quilt becomes something for the people remaining—a memento that provides comfort and emotional support.

Planning a memory quilt is a collaborative effort. My clients and I generally begin our planning meeting by looking at the textiles they want to incorporate into their project. Then we examine my portfolio. Looking at the projects I've made for others helps people focus on what they want for themselves. By looking at all of this, they're better able to see all the possibilities. The end product is definitely a composite of my client's vision and my artistic input. My clients tell me how big they want it, whether it's going on the wall or on the back of a couch or on a bed, whether it's going to be something to look at or whether it's going to be functional, and from there I go off on my own.

My very first commissioned memory quilt was made in 1986 for the AIDS NAMES project. I was asked to make a quilt to honor the memory of a friend's younger brother who had recently died of AIDS. Butch had been active in Republican politics, did magic tricks and had been a volunteer at the local fire station, so his quilt panel has those three images on it.

One time a woman arrived at my studio with several bags filled with colorful scarves that had belonged to her mother, who had recently died. She had decided to honor her mother's memory by transforming the many scarves—her mother's fashion trademark— into decorative pillows. I had free license to combine the scarves into a "crazy quilt" design. Scarves for each of the pillows were grouped together based on their colors, patterns, and the scale of their designs, resulting in beautiful pillows that reflected the vibrant personality of the woman who wore them.

I've made a memory quilt that included a collection of Harley-Davidson T-shirts for a woman whose late husband had a passion for his Harley-Davidson. I've made memory pillows for the widow of an avid golfer, using fabric and labels from his many golf shirts, as well as logos from the golf clubs where he played. I've also made a collection of coordinated memory pillows out of five cable-knit sweaters that had belonged to a client's mother, along with a cozy lap blanket made from her jeans, denim jacket, and other articles of clothing. Another time, a widow with two adult sons told me she wanted pillows made from her husband's collection of silk ties. She had carefully separated them into piles of gold and harvest tones, blues, and deep reds, point-ing out which ties she wanted included in each pillow. Then she gifted two of them to her sons and saved the third for herself.

Several years ago I made a very large quilt—six feet by eight feet— for a man whose wife had died three years earlier. He arrived at my studio with two large bags of his wife's clothing and cautioned me to not wash or dry-clean any of the textiles because, in his words, "They still have her fragrance on them." I couldn't detect any fragrance, but he wanted to make sure that it remained. As he took out each piece of

Memory quilt by Eileen Belmont.

clothing, he commented about its history—where they had purchased it, when she had worn it, why it was her favorite, and why he wanted it included in the quilt. He wanted his quilt to be large enough so that he and his three young children could comfortably snuggle under it whenever they watched a movie together.

I've worked on several hundred projects in the last five years and I think the biggest surprise to me in all this is that I find myself in another zone when I'm working on a memorial quilt. It's a very different process from working on a project that celebrates a college graduation, a wedding anniversary, a first communion, or a bar mitzvah. Totally different. I'm generally pretty bubbly, but this work puts me in a different mental zone because it's a reverential process. I get teary—these people have saved these textiles and it means the world to them. How could I not get teary when someone says to me, "My wife was wearing this on our first date," or "My wife loved to cook and these are four aprons that she always wore and please don't wash them even though they have stains on them"? Every component piece has meaning. That's what's so special about this.

My own mother died Thanksgiving weekend 2007. I saved some of her clothing . . . and I still can't do anything with it. It feels too raw. I can't give her things away, but I can't work with them yet either. My mother wore these things. Sometimes, when I describe to people what I do, they're repulsed by the idea of taking the clothing of a deceased person and making a quilt or decorative pillow or wall hanging out of it, but other people say it's such a beautiful thing to be able to do. My feeling is, if it works for someone, then it's the right thing to do. It's a comfort to the people who are going to use it or look at it; they can handle the textiles. When they look at it, they might say, "I remember when Mom wore that dress" or "I remember when my wife wore that" or "This is what grandma gave me for my fifteenth birthday." It maintains the connection they have with that person, which is so very important.

"The Funniest Woman You've Never Heard Of"

— as shared by Gary Toll

Gary Toll is a filmmaker who works on both coasts. He was born in Philadelphia and studied film at Temple University. After graduation he went into business and became involved in a number of ventures, including used car sales and real estate development. Following the death of his sister—writer, actress, and standup comic Judy Toll—from cancer at the age of forty-four in 2002, Toll and his family moved to Los Angeles so that he could pursue a career in film. Judy Toll: The Funniest Woman You've Never Heard Of—*a 2008 documentary about the life of his sister, written and directed by him—has received critical acclaim and won numerous film festival awards.*

Gary Toll

৪৩

As CHILDREN, JUDY AND I WOULD PLAY a game we called "Make Me Laugh." I was probably eight or nine at the time, and Judy was a

Judy and Gary Toll

couple of years older than I. We would play characters and dress up in crazy costumes, all to try to make each other laugh. We would laugh so loud that it often woke our father, who would get very angry since he had to get up early in the morning to work in his furniture store in downtown Philly. We were always getting into trouble.

Judy and I always had a close, unusual bond. When we would go anywhere with the family, she and I would start interacting with each other, kind of like the "cone of silence" from *Get Smart*. It was as if the cone came down around us and no one else was around. We were always laughing, and Judy was the leader of all things fun and funny. If we weren't laughing, there was definitely something wrong.

In the late sixties and early seventies, Judy and I began performing in musicals for a local charity group called Women's American ORT. They were big musical productions and were a very influential part of our lives and our futures. We loved the theater and loved the stage. We both performed in high school musicals and did shows in college, and, after Judy graduated from the University of Massachusetts, we teamed up and did a standup act. There were several new standup clubs around Philadelphia where we did open mic nights until we got regular gigs. One of our favorite bits, which Judy wrote, was "The Reader's Digest Condensed Version of *The Wizard of Oz.*" She was great at that. She knew all the words to all the songs and could sing them at lightning speed. I would add characters in between the songs and we would do the whole movie in under two minutes. Judy was an extremely hard worker and I was eighteen or nineteen at the time and not as serious as Judy so eventually she fired me. After a year or so, Judy had gotten pretty popular in the Philadelphia comedy scene and she decided to move to LA.

Several years after Judy moved to LA and started to make a name for herself, our younger sister, Joanne, moved there. At that point I was married with a daughter still living on the East Coast, so moving to the West Coast to get into show business was not an option. I was no stranger to filmmaking, as I had been making movies since I was fourteen using a Super 8 film camera. So, when video came out in the eighties, I bought a giant video camera with a backpack and a VCR player. Whenever Joanne came to Philadelphia, we made a movie about Judy, and whenever Judy came, we made a movie about Joanne. We would watch our movies over and over and just laugh till it hurt. We still do, but it's not the same without Judy.

Judy's whole act and whole life was about being brutally honest. I loved and admired that about Judy and I try to live my life that way. One of the funniest things about Judy is that she was always getting into trouble. Her friends often said that Judy would get herself into crazy situations just so she would have something to write about. She was a Scientologist for a year and she would write about it. She was one of the writers for *Sex and the City* and a lot of those stories came from her life. Judy used to do a thing in LA called the "Uncab," which stands for "Uncabaret." The Uncab was a venue for comics to get up and talk about what was going on in their lives. Judy would tell stories like the time she walked into a *Sex and the City* writers' meeting and said, "I've got a great idea," and then proceeded to tell them a story from her life. The other writers would say, "That *is* a great idea." And Judy would never let on that it was based on something that actually happened to her.

Sadly, I had a warm-up to her death. Six months before she died, our father died. It was very rough—he was sixty-seven at the time, living in Florida and enjoying his retirement. The stress of Judy's cancer was tough on all of us, but it was especially hard on Dad and one day he fell on the golf course and hurt his shoulder. When he went for x-rays, they found a spot on his lung and needed to see if it was cancer. He had smoked for many years and didn't eat well—he was not the healthiest guy. He looked nervous going into surgery, and I asked, "What are you afraid of?" He said, "I'm afraid of dying." I told him he had nothing to be afraid of and I went back to work. I have always regretted saying that. During the surgery, they removed the right upper lobe of his lung, which apparently was standard procedure, but his heart was too weak to recover and shortly after the surgery he had two heart attacks and triple bypass surgery, got pneumonia, and died after a five-week battle. Judy was undergoing cancer treatments at the time and was unable to fly in for his funeral. Although it was out of her control, Judy felt horrible for missing her father's funeral.

After going through the death of my father, my world shifted and nothing was ever going to be the same, and that's still true to this day. The only thing I could do at that point was go through the motions. I pictured myself breaking down and running away but there were too many other people involved. My mother had just lost her husband of forty-five years and was about to lose her first-born child. I knew I had to be strong for her and the family. My wife, my daughter, my cousins—the least I could do was put on a good show for them.

So I went through the motions with my father and six weeks later I got a devastating phone call. I remember it vividly—a voice said, "This is the nurse at John Wayne Cancer Institute in Los Angeles, California, and we need you to come out here right away." I still get nauseous just thinking about it. I mean, what do you say to that? It's just harsh. I called my wife and told her what the nurse said, and my wife said we needed to get our daughter out of school and fly to LA.

We arrived the next day and went straight to the hospital. All of the people who knew and loved Judy, her friends and family—just about everyone was there. Judy was on a respirator and unconscious, so we went to her bedside one at a time to say goodbye. Most of the people who were there were entertainers and comedy people, so a lot of funny things were said, and plenty of tears were shed.

Judy was pretty much loved by everyone. We have a picture on our dresser of Judy giving then-President Bill Clinton a big hug. When she approached him, the secret service stepped in to stop her, but President Clinton said, "No, it's okay. It's Judy."

Making the Judy movie was difficult, especially in the beginning. It took us over three years to make the film. We moved to LA six years ago with the idea to work in the business, learn the tricks of the trade and then make this movie. I gathered up all her material but could only watch for five minutes at a time because I would break down, but it got easier as time went on. I knew how to make movies but it had been many years, so I went to LA film school for a year. When we started working together on the Judy movie and other people were watching and laughing, that made me feel good and I knew we could make something great.

My goal was always to get people to know and love Judy like we did. It was always my conviction that, for some weird reason, the universe didn't recognize Judy. She was incredibly talented and loved by all the heavy hitters in Hollywood—in California I'm known as Judy's brother—so there was no reason that she shouldn't be very successful and very famous. Not to say she wasn't successful, because she was, but she was known as a writer and what she most wanted was to be an actor. It always bugged me that she wasn't better known. And most people come away from the movie saying *I wish I knew her*. People should see Judy and enjoy her. "To share her humor with the world"—that's the closing line of the movie, and I'm the one who says it.

CHAPTER 6

Appreciating Our Troops

— as shared by the Wolfer Family

O*n April 6, 2008, Major Stuart Adam Wolfer was killed while serving in Iraq—in the Green Zone in Baghdad. Wolfer leaves behind his wife, Lee, and daughters Lillian, Melissa, and Izzy. To honor his memory and enable his legacy to continue to live on and inspire future generations, his parents—Esther and Len Wolfer—and sister—Beverly Wolfer-Nerenberg—created the Major Stuart Adam Wolfer Institute (MSAWI).*

Stuart Adam Wolfer

MSAWI (www.msawi.org) is dedicated to connecting the American community with the U.S. military. MSAWI supports U.S. troops stationed abroad and domestically. Through educational programs at schools, community centers, and religious institutions, MSAWI seeks to increase public awareness of the sacrifices that U.S. servicepeople make every day on our behalf.

&

As the news of Stuart's tragic death spread among family, friends, military, and business colleagues, we [his parents and sister] began to receive an outpouring of emails and notes sharing with us how Stuart affected each of their lives. We knew how special Stuart was to us, his family. What we did not know in such depth was how much Stuart meant to other people and the difference he made in their lives. Stuart touched people's lives in big and small ways.

Stuart was a remarkable man. During his job interview for his most recent position with Thomson West of Thomson Reuters, Stuart listed his core values to his to-be hiring manager: God, family, country, duty, friendship, and lastly, self. If he was hired, he said, he would remain committed to his values and that he would not let his manager down. Stuart was a man of his word.

As we were preparing for a memorial program in Stuart's memory, we realized that when a dandelion dies it does not simply shrivel up and fall on the ground but rather turns white, and when you blow it, its seeds scatter to the far ends of the earth to begin anew. We do *not* believe that Stuart died to simply be buried in this earth. We believe that, like the dandelion, Stuart's seeds of teaching will continue to touch those of us who learn about him. We refuse to allow Stuart's voice to be silenced. We decided then that we needed to establish an organization in Stuart's memory.

MSAWI seeks to directly involve local communities in its mission so that those of us at home give of our most precious resource—our *time*. In the work that we do, we often feel Stuart's presence. I [Stuart's mom, Esther] have always loved butterflies. Sometimes when we are at a memorial program or just having a rough day, a butterfly will fly by and I know that Stuart is watching me . . . helping me. It is his way of coming by to say hello and to urge on me and my family. To me, the dandelion is my butterfly.

When we receive letters from soldiers detailing the impact a care package made on them, we know that Stuart would be proud. That everyday Americans, regardless of their political views, took the time to think of and support the troops overseas.

Stuart's untimely death continues to haunt us with many unanswered questions. A day does not go by that we do not think of him. We sometimes find ourselves reaching for the phone to call him to just catch up, as it has been a while. Then our new reality comes crashing back at us. Yet, having MSAWI allows us a positive outlet for expressing our grief, for remembering and honoring Stuart and for helping others. Our lives have been forever changed, yet if we can demonstrate our appreciation to deployed troops and enlighten Americans about the sacrifices of our brave men and women in the U.S. military, then we will have honored Stuart.

Logo of MSAWI.

CHAPTER 7

Work, Altruism, Spirituality

— as shared by Liz and Steve Alderman

Liz and Steve Alderman of Westchester, New York, set up the Peter C. Alderman Foundation (www.petercaldermanfounda-tion.org) to honor the memory of their twenty-five-year-old son, who was killed on 9/11 at the World Trade Center. In the past seven years, the foundation has trained 385 doctors in twenty countries on four continents and opened nine mental health clinics to treat posttraumatic stress disorder (PTSD) and mental depression in countries such as Rwanda, Haiti, Uganda, and Cambodia. The foundation-trained

Peter C. Alderman
[COURTESY OF PETER C. ALDERMAN FOUNDATION.]

staff has treated more than one hundred thousand patients and has partnerships with the governments of Rwanda, Angola, and Cambodia. Barron's named the foundation one of the ten best small foundations or charities in the United States. The Aldermans received the Purpose Prize, which honors American social entrepreneurs over the age of sixty.

ॐ

SHORTLY AFTER HE DIED, his friends needed to be together and to be with us. So his friends got in cars from all over the country and drove here. We ended up having over 250 of his friends at our home a week and a day after he died.

His hobby was relationships. He was not the honor student who became an honor student after he died. His brother, who is six years older, said when I grow up I want to be like Pete. In fact, we have an arm of the foundation called Friends of Peter Alderman. These kids every year get together and raise money for the foundation. They raise a lot of money. They just had a walk-a-thon that netted over seventy thousand dollars. These are his friends and they are still part of our lives. The tough part is, we are invited to their weddings and they bring their children to see us. It's very difficult, but we would still rather have them in our lives than not.

We knew we had to create our own memorial for Peter. We really didn't know what to do. And then we saw a *Nightline* broadcast that said one billion people in this world—one-sixth of humanity—have directly experienced torture terrorism and, of those who have survived, over 50 percent suffer debilitating traumatic depression and posttraumatic stress disorder. They can't work, children can't go to school, and some people can't even leave their beds.

There was nothing we could do for Peter, but if we could return the survivors of terrorism to life, then that would be the perfect memorial because Peter so loved life.

We are building and contributing significantly to the evidence that tells us that psychiatry in postconflict countries is at the center of recovery. On a personal level, the work is terribly, terribly important. It is a reason to get out of bed every morning and function at a high level. We feel really, really good about the people we are able to help and the doctors we are meeting along the way.

The main reason for starting this is that we wanted to leave a mark that Peter existed on this earth. He died at a very young age. We believe that we have left a profound and indelible mark that Peter existed; the world is a better place because he lived. Peter loved life and if we can return people to life so that they can live their lives, that is the perfect way to memorialize him.

It's important work. We never dreamed that we would do something so huge and so incredibly effective. We just followed this path and, through a lot of passion and very, very hard work, this is where we are today. It takes up every bit of our time, seven days a week, ten to twelve hours a day.

We traveled all across northern Uganda to visit our clinics and held a conference in Kampala—our second conference—to train doctors from Africa. Last year we invited 40 doctors and 84 doctors came from ten East African countries. This year 216 doctors came from eleven countries. This is really growing and it's our way of training doctors to deal with this particular problem.

We never traveled before. This has profoundly changed the trajectory of our lives—the way we live and think and see the world. We will not allow that anything good came from our son's death, but it certainly changed a number of things in our lives, our mindset and outlook on life.

We knew nothing about the world of philanthropy. This was all brand-new to us, but if you have the passion to do something and the will to work hard, you can do anything. We didn't have a clue what we were doing when we started, and we still are learning. With passion and narrow focus and hard work, anybody can accomplish anything. We're not special people.

One of our partners, the Harvard Program of Refugee Trauma, did a yearlong study in an internal displaced persons camp. Everyone in the camp had been traumatized at least as much as we had and maybe even more so by the loss of loved ones or loss of their homes. Many of the mothers had seen their children starve to death in their arms and many had seen husbands led away to be executed. They interviewed one thousand households. People were depressed, suicide was rampant, alcoholism was rampant, there was spousal abuse, child abuse—everything bad that could happen, happened. There were three very powerful things that militated against bad behavior—spirituality, work, and altruism. People were as upset as before but they did not dwell on it. They did not have time to obsess about it because they were concentrating on something else. These were powerful means for avoiding depression, and the people who did this were a lot healthier, a lot better off than those who didn't.

Work, altruism, and spirituality—we combine all of that in our clinics everywhere. We are not faith-based, but all of our patients in Cambodia go to the local monastery, where they are seen each week and then followed for a year afterward to watch out for any recidivism. That is really important because most believe that if they are depressed, it is because the gods are angry with them.

We only train and work with indigenous people. We have received e-mails from retired psychologists and psychiatrists saying they would love to work in our clinics. We can't do it. When you are working with mental health, if it is not culturally appropriate, it won't work. We are training people to deal with their own local population.

Traumatic depression and PTSD in Africa are more prevalent than HIV/AIDS, TB, and malaria combined.

We hear all the time, "Why are you dealing with mental health when there are so many other pressing problems in the world, like hunger and diseases?" Our answer is that good mental health is essential to all of this. Billions of dollars are being spent on HIV/AIDS and other diseases, but if people don't care whether they live or die, they will not bother to

Aldermans with President Obama. [COURTESY OF PETER C. ALDERMAN FOUNDATION]

take medication and walk an extra mile for potable water. They will just reach outside their hut and drink the water that is running outside their door. If you can't get out of bed, you're not going to be able to take advantage of the micro loans that are being made. We believe mental health is essential to postconflict recovery.

CHAPTER 8

Keeping Memories Fresh and Green

— as shared by Nick Clooney

---

*Nick Clooney has been a colum-
nist for the* Cincinnati Post, *a
television news anchor for the
ABC affiliate in Cincinnati, and
the host of the 1970s ABC game
show* The Money Maze. *He has
worked on other television sta-
tions in Los Angeles, Salt Lake
City, and Buffalo, and in the
1990s could be seen hosting*
American Movie Classics. *He
has taught courses on journalism
and film at American University
and is the author of* The Movies
That Changed Us: Reflections
on the Screen.
*Clooney is the brother of the
late singers Rosemary and Betty Clooney and the father of actor George
Clooney. Following Betty's death at the age of forty-five from brain
trauma caused by an aneurysm, Nick and Rosemary established the Betty*

Nick Clooney
[WITH PERMISSION FROM NICK CLOONEY
FROM *NICK: COLLECTED COLUMNS OF NICK
CLOONEY.*]

Clooney Foundation (1983) and the Betty Clooney Center (1988) to address the needs of survivors of traumatic brain injury. In addition, the legacy of social responsibility passed down by Nick's grandfather Andrew Clooney lives on in a third generation with Nick's son George, with whom Nick traveled to Darfur in 2006 to film a documentary about the genocide taking place there.

☎

I'M NOT SURE I HAVE COPED with the loss of my sisters. They seem very much a part of me even now. We were Depression kids and were each other's resources and there was no opportunity for us to think of being separate from each other. We knew that the one relationship that would always work was this brother-sister relationship. We could always count on each other; the rest of the world was pretty shaky at that time. Our mother and father had separated and we were raised by our grandmother and we moved quite a bit. I went to thirteen schools. I'm sure Rosemary and Betty went to a similar number. But what stayed constant through all of that was our absolute dependence upon one another and our absolute affection for one another. That I could count on until the very moment of the deaths of both of them—Betty very early on and Rosemary only a couple of years ago.

Rosemary and Betty Clooney.
[WITH PERMISSION FROM NICK CLOONEY FROM *NICK: COLLECTED COLUMNS OF NICK CLOONEY*.]

When they died it was wrenching, obviously. Betty was so young —only in her mid-forties when she died. And Rosemary, although she was in her seventies, was my only remaining full sister. That was the final breakup of what used to be known in our family as the Clooney kids. I'm the last one standing and one of my duties—and a very pleasant duty—is to make sure as best I can that the memories of both of my sisters remain fresh and green, particularly to those who did not know them. So I do whatever I can to make sure that that works.

How do I do that? There are these music specials on PBS that are done regularly and I'll host if Rosemary or Betty is in them. The fact that Betty left us so early makes it more difficult but more imperative that people not forget that she was also a world-class singer and a television pioneer, and not only in Cincinnati. She was the first female co-host on the *Today* show with John Chancellor. It lasted only a short period of time because John Chancellor was not at all happy with having anyone on that program who did not have a news background. So it was not necessarily a happy experience, but it was a pioneering experience. And Betty worked *The Morning Show* with Jack Paar on CBS before Jack had his great success on NBC with *The Tonight Show*. She was a singer on his morning program as well.

My fondest memories are the personal ones, the times we were together. Betty was the funniest woman who ever lived. She wasn't funny by telling jokes. She didn't say funny things—she said things funny and she would make us helpless with laughter to the point where we could hardly breathe. Any time I could be with them or have them with me, we did it. I had a variety show in Cincinnati for a number of years and whenever I could get the budget I would have both Rosemary and Betty or one or the other in to co-host with me for a week or two so we could do this together. I have a couple of specials that I pull out every now and then and look at them just to remember how special it was to be their brother.

The genesis of all of this was in Maysville, Kentucky, where the three of us were born and our grandmother raised us. I somehow knew—actually Rosemary and Betty knew more than I—that they were going to be in the entertainment business and I, on the other hand, was focused on the magic voices that came out of the radio. We would go to the Russell Theater on Saturday afternoons and stay all day. We'd watch the double feature and the cartoon and newsreel and when we came home we were those people. If it was *Girl Friday*, I was Cary Grant and Rosemary would be Rosalind Russell and Betty would be Ralph Bellamy. We would do the dialogue.

We had Sunday specials in our family with everybody—aunts and uncles would all come to the house up on Third Street for Sunday dinner—and we used the doorway between the dining room and the living room as the proscenium arch and everybody had to perform. You had to sing or dance or do something. That was part of the family ritual and we would all do something from the movies. Rosemary would sing a song and Betty would sing a song or dance and they would use me as the comedy foil. That is what we did and somehow it got into our heads that this is what we were going to do. This was when I was five, Betty was eight, and Rosemary was eleven. But Rosemary and Betty were singing together from the time they were six and three, doing talent shows in Maysville. We used to have a saying—musicians would understand this—if Rosemary belched, Betty had a third for it. In the meantime I was listening to Gabriel Heatter on the radio and Ed Murrow.

Rosemary and Betty went to work when they were thirteen and sixteen on WLW, which was the biggest station in the Midwest at the time. By the time I was sixteen, I was in Maysville and walked up to WFTM—the world's finest tobacco market—and I knocked on the door and said I want to be in radio. They thought I was terrific and I went to work. I worked during high school and then full time, and after basic training in the service I ended up in Germany with the American Forces Network.

All of that was born of the assumption—it's incredible to think of it now—that we would be able to do this out of Maysville, Kentucky. But the interesting thing about small towns—their real value—is that they are so small, and if you have a modicum of talent, the people around the town think you're wonderful. They begin to give you a certain amount of confidence and tell you that you ought to be in radio and the movies. By the time you get to the big town and find out that you're not maybe as great as they said, you're already working because you had enough confidence to take you farther than others. And the guys and women who can work themselves out of the great urban areas and get to the top, I admire tremendously. Those of us coming from smaller communities had it much easier.

Rosemary's career was just a rocket—it was cosmic. But we all did pretty well, and it all came out of this little tiny town and it just seemed that there never was any question about what we were going to do. And it was led by the courage and the talent of my two sisters. And when their careers took off and I began to do reasonably well, too, we would talk about it and wonder how it happened.

It was the hard work and the ability to get back up again; we somehow understood that. You keep reinventing yourself and find out what you do best and how it might be useful to an audience. Rosemary and Betty did all of those things and because they did, I did, too. So here I am, seventy-five years old and they are still paying me to do this stuff. I can't believe it.

We also have a family legacy of social responsibility. It was Poppa [grandfather] Clooney who first made us aware that we're connected to the world beyond Maysville and that we have a responsibility to that world. In the long reach of things, he was a pompous guy. He didn't like kids much and we adored him. He talked to us like we were short adults. When I was five, he talked to me about Russia, the New Deal and that the incinerator in Maysville was a great thing, an improvement from the garbage dump that had been there before. He talked to us with polemics and he wrote wonderfully and was self-educated. He once took me to the Ohio River and had me put my hand in the water. He had already done this with Rosemary and Betty, who were down there, too. They smiled smugly because it had already happened to them. When I got my hand in the Ohio River, he said, "Nicholas, the water that touches your hand will reach the channel and go down to Cairo, Illinois, and down the Mississippi, past New Orleans, and into the Gulf. It will then be picked up by the Gulf Stream and from there swept around the Florida peninsula and from there it would be taken on ship bottoms all around the world. So, Nicholas," he said, "you are no longer a small-town boy. You are connected to the world from this point on and you will go to many of those places and do many big things in your lifetime. I have only one piece of advice—always remember where you put your hand in the water."

He broadened our horizons from this little place. He himself seldom got out of Maysville. He was a small-town mayor. He was the mayor of the city and was still running the year he died. We had always—Rosemary and Betty and I—always felt we were part of a bigger world and that certainly was a residue of our grandfather's thought process. The rest of the family was more concerned with parochial issues of what's going on in Maysville. So he certainly gave us the sense that there was something else out there.

That sense of being part of something larger certainly lives on in George. When it came to Darfur, George and I were talking and he pointed me to the articles that Nick Kristof was writing in the *New York Times*. I knew of the Sudan and the war that had been going on there for twenty years, but I didn't know that Darfur was the western part of Sudan until George pointed this out. George and I talked about it for six months and he said, "The cameras are following me everywhere because I'm reasonably hot at the moment. What happens if we go over there?" The State Department didn't want us there and the CIA definitely didn't, but we were able to pull it together as a private enterprise—just four of us in an old Cessna popping in from south Sudan. George said I'll be the shooter and you be the reporter. And that is what we did. But he's a really smart guy, so he did some reporting, too, and some stand-ups and some of the interviews. I did a batch of them as well. This was in April 2006 and we got back in time to be part of a rally on a Sunday. Because of George it was a huge rally —not five thousand, but fifty thousand came. President Bush got a peace agreement on May 5, but we didn't know that everybody could sign on and nobody does a thing about it.

So we kept at it and did a documentary about it and it was shown around the world. And George went to the UN with Elie Wiesel and I thought they did a wonderful speech to the Security Council. I'm now out talking to colleges and high schools—three hundred speeches in these three years—everything from three hundred thousand people to fifty. I'm trying to make it a priority—instead of number twenty, to move it up to seventeen. We figure we owe it to the innocent victims who are caught in the crossfire. And we'll continue to do it. I think Poppa Clooney would have wanted us to.

The Betty Clooney Foundation for Persons with Brain Injuries in Long Beach, California, was founded in the early 1980s. It had a lot of help from the state and turned into a very useful resource in Southern California. It was terrific. And of course we did benefits, anything we could do from progressive dinners to a big thing at the Dorothy Chandler Pavilion, where we did a singers' salute to songwriters. I was the emcee and Rosemary was the hostess and brought in entertainers and filled the place up for five or six years. It gave some measure of notoriety to the cause for people with brain injuries—the silent epidemic that's out there. It has had to constrict its efforts in recent years because money has dried up. It's one of those things that every foundation has to face.

Rosemary had a home here in Augusta, Kentucky. Because [wife] Nina and I were here, she bought a house because she wanted to be as close as she could to us. Nina fixed it up and Rosemary spent about one-third of her year here. Any time she was in the east, this was her headquarters. After she died, the house went to her children. It was later purchased by Steve Henry—a former lieutenant governor here—and his wife, Heather, and they put together a wonderful museum saluting Rosemary. We provided all the artifacts we could. It's open year-round.

Meantime, every September we have a Rosemary Clooney Music Festival in Maysville. They perform right downtown where Rosemary and Betty first performed trying to get a crowd when our grandpa was running for office. They would sing songs and gather fifteen or twenty people around and then grandpa would magically appear from a doorway and hand out cards saying, "I'm Andrew Clooney and I'm running for mayor." I remember the first one of these festivals. I was the emcee and of course Rosemary was the focus and it was a wonderful event. And Rosemary looked at the crowd and said, "This was where I started my career—at Third and Market singing for nothing. Now, seventy years later, I'm at Third and Market and still singing for nothing."

Betty would have been such a great old lady. That's a reason I'm still steamed at her for dying. She would be seventy-eight now, and she would have the funniest take on all of us—on Rosemary and Nina; she loved my wife, Nina, and me. She would have sent us up forever; we wouldn't be able to catch our breath. We wouldn't have time to die, we'd be laughing too hard.

I don't think anybody requires advice on how to move beyond mourning, except maybe they need to be reminded of it. Think of all the wonderful things. As soon as that awful wrench occurs and the person you love in the deepest corner of your heart breathes his or her last, move as quickly as you can past that to the great funny, uplifting moments you shared with them. And if you are able to take that positive energy—say it's a high-profile person like Rosemary or Betty—and move it toward something that they would be proud to be associated with, then do it. Take that positive energy and create, let us say, one scholarship, one one-thousand-dollar scholarship in your high school named for the person you loved so much. And you go to the high school and say, "I want someone who couldn't go to a state college without this to have it and I want it every year until I'm gone." Maybe it is something smaller than that—maybe it's a dinner for senior citizens that your loved one would really appreciate. And every time you present the dinner, tell them "I'm doing this because I loved my uncle. He was a great fellow and I wish you had known him." So do something to remember them positively in the world because you have to know, whatever your beliefs are, that they are resting much easier because you did that.

The great love you have for the people who have impacted your life should mean something. Rosemary used to say when somebody would die—Betty said this, too, but Rosemary had a phrase for it— when somebody who meant so much to her died, she would say three or four months later, maybe a year later, "Boy, the water closed over him very quickly, didn't it." And she would look distressed at that. And I remembered that and I wanted to make sure that the water didn't close quickly over Rosemary or Betty.

CHAPTER 9

The Sock Puppet That Launched a Career

— as shared by Ronn Lucas

Ronn Lucas has been a ventriloquist for forty-five of his fifty-five years. Inspired by a sock puppet with which his grandfather entertained his grandchildren, he has gone on to perform for several U.S. presidents and the Queen of England. He has appeared on numerous TV shows, including The Late Show with David Letterman *and* The Tonight Show with Jay Leno, *had his own TV show in Great Britain, and performs in Las Vegas and on cruise lines. Lucas incorporates the living memory of his grandfather into every show by presenting a tribute to the man who launched his career with a sock puppet.*

※

WE HAD A TRADITION OF GATHERING at the Tully family house. My real name is Ronny Wayne Tully. Grandpa Tully had a very dry sense of humor. I had three sets of grandparents—the Tullys, the Connors, and the Lucases. The Lucases are my stepfamily. My mom remarried and they all lived in the same farming community and a lot of the stories I tell are an amalgam because all three sets of grandparents supported my creativity and what I was trying to do.

Ronn Lucas with his puppet family.
[PHOTO COURTESY OF RONN LUCAS.]

The ending in my act, where I talk about my grandpa, is one of several endings I have. The story goes like this: We had spent ten hours driving across Texas at Christmastime and we arrived at midnight at my grandparents' house. My grandma had made hot chocolate and went to bed and my granddad waited up for us. They had a Christmas tree and presents and I was all sleepy and cranky and Grandpa took a Christmas stocking off the mantelpiece and upended it and turned it into a puppet. It was a very powerful thing. As a kid you learn that adults aren't like you and it's interesting when you find an adult who thinks like you do—who has an approach to life like a kid does. He came up with the idea of having cardboard bodies for the sock puppets, like a rabbit and a turtle. He made a lot of them for my cousins and me and I think I have the last one.

We found an old photograph in which I'm sitting on the steps with a couple of cousins, and Grandpa is standing there with a puppet and is holding forth for us. The ventriloquism came later. I was sitting with another set of grandparents watching television and Edgar Bergen was on. I asked what that was and was told he was a ventriloquist. I never met Edgar Bergen but I found out years later that he had a really good technique but had to let it go for radio to get the pronunciation right. Transmission quality wasn't really great, so it was really important to enunciate. So he couldn't use the substitutions we normally do and let his lips go in order to make Charlie sound alive.

By the time I was eight, I had my first store-bought dummy from, I think, a Montgomery Ward catalogue. It was a plastic Danny O'Day doll—you may remember Jimmy Nelson who did the Nestle commercials. I would spend summers with the Connors, and my grandmother Connor would make little costumes and shirts, pants, and jackets for my character. He had a great wardrobe.

I learned ventriloquism from a book and from the ventriloquists who appeared on TV, like Jerry Lane and Señor Wences, Jimmy Nelson, Paul Winchell, and Shari Lewis. I never thought I'd make a career of this. I'm fifty-five. I've been doing it for forty-five years and professionally for thirty-five years. I refer to it as a hobby that got out of hand.

Grandpa was not a ventriloquist, but it fired some neurons in my brain. It was like a little explosion in my imagination—that it's okay to grow up and do something like that. I had support for this from my grandparents but not at all from my parents. In fact, not too long ago I received a lifetime achievement award from the ventriloquist world. I invited my parents and I told my mom that when I get this out of my system, I'll go back to college. Nobody in my family is in show business and so they have no clue how I do what I do or why I do what I do.

I gave up college to do this. I was at the University of Texas for two years and then I ran out of money. So I thought, I'll skip a semester and go to work and I've been performing ever since. I haven't always had the work I've wanted, but I have never not worked as an entertainer.

The best advice I ever got was from another great father figure, Bill Cosby. He told me, "Never leave your wallet in the dressing room." And that's been pretty much it.

To me, my grandparents are still around. I'm sort of a representation of what they are. Through forty-eight thousand years of evolution, we, as a human species, had an oral tradition; we passed things on. Technology has sort of taken that away from us as adults. But for kids, the imagination is wide open and anything you do is okay. You don't have to be a good puppeteer; if you move your lips, it doesn't matter. If you're trying to connect your imagination to theirs, they're so willing to go along for the ride.

My grandmother Connor used to read to me, sometimes just from the Bible. She was a very religious lady. Other times she read stories from Greek mythology and Aesop's Fables. I think it's interesting that when you do this, you don't talk down to kids—you talk to them.

Why did I add the ending about my grandfather and the puppet? Well, I had the routine for a while and it seemed incomplete . . . like it was lacking heart. And then I realized there was something to share about how it came about. Just building a puppet out of socks was kind of cool, but there was a backstory about how I learned it and why. And to do the comedy and to tag it at the end was good theater, which is all about communicating and reaching people on a visceral level. That's what the routine itself was lacking, and so I decided to tell the story about my grandfather. It resonates with the audience because I set up a premise and then it goes into comedy, but at the end I return to the premise. Sometimes, when you share something, it doesn't die even if you do.

His name was Alvin Tully. I really, really miss him, but I gloss over it. He died when I was in my thirties—twenty years ago, when he was in his late seventies. He was a lay minister and he obviously spoke very well. I never got to watch him preach. They didn't have an actual minister at their church. The minister probably got called to another church and they were waiting for a new one to come in. It was a small rural community and occasionally people would get up and talk. My grandfather was the guy who would conduct the service. He wasn't an ordained minister and wasn't receiving any funding, but he was a recognized elder in his church. He was religious and so was my grandmother.

I think magic exists as a perception and he had a way of sharing magic. I tried doing evangelism with my puppetry but was never comfortable with it.

My grandfather was in the Church of Christ. In the opening announcements in my show in Las Vegas, my puppet reminds the audience that there might be some extremely mild adult language in the show, so if the kind of words used by third and fourth graders on the playground are offensive to you, you might be Southern Baptists and you should stay out of the casino. So I poke fun at my roots.

I had been at the Rio for eight years and I'm now working at the Excalibur. My main character is a dragon puppet who fits the castle motif extremely well. I don't bring him on cruise ships because he breathes fire. He has a fire generator and there is smokeless black powder. And when I travel with him, he registers at the airport as if he's a weapon.

Billy's fine. Billy's my roots. The cowboy puppet was definitely the kid I wanted to be—the know-it-all, smart-aleck kid who got away with everything.

I named the hand puppet George. My grandfather named his hand puppets, but they were all biblical names. I'm thinking Shadrach, Meshach, and Abednego. He didn't do Bible tales but he was a very religious man, a very sweet man. He was a very hardworking man. When they went off baling hay, it was amazing how much work they did and they didn't say anything. Even if you were hurting, complaining just wasn't done in Texas. None of this, "Oy, my back." You just didn't do that.

I come from a culture in Texas where people had that pioneer ethic and suffered silently. For him to do something like this was just way out of the blue for anybody and yet nobody thought anything about it. It was just his nature. He was using everyday household objects and making a lot of something out of nothing. And that, I think, is an interesting legacy.

I did this performance for Queen Elizabeth with socks and she asked me after the show, "Do you have any more talking laundry at home?" After that, I started joking that "Grandpa talked to a lot of laundry but we just don't go into that." That's a line I took from Her Majesty Queen Elizabeth II.

CHAPTER 10

"The Rock of Our Family"

— as shared by Jeanette Martinez

Jeanette Martinez is an education technician in North Carolina, where she lives with her husband, Bill, a retired career marine. While stationed in Okinawa, they went to Korea to adopt their first daughter, Melissa. Their other daughter, Jessica, who has Down syndrome, is a featured extra in "A Smile as Big as the Moon," a Hallmark Hall of Fame Productions *movie that aired on ABC in January 2012.*

આ

My mother thought I should already know I'm loved, so she never said it and I never felt like I was good enough, but as a grandmother there was none better. It wasn't until I had children that I realized just how special my mom was. Then she moved here to North Carolina and we finally started building a relationship, but she only lived here five years before she was taken from us.

If I had to pick one special moment, I guess it was when my youngest was born. Jessica was born on October 1 at 7:37 in the morning, and at 7:45 the doctors came in and told me she had Down syndrome. I went through the five stages of mourning because I was mourning the dream that every mother has when they're pregnant—a

Caroline Vargas with grandchildren Jessica and Melissa Martinez.

child's college graduation, her wedding, having grandchildren—and now I would have none of that. I cried for three days and doubted that God knew what He was doing, giving me a child like this. I called my mom and told her I thought I should put my baby up for adoption because I would not be a good mother to a special-needs child. I'll never forget what she said to me. In the calmest, most loving voice I ever heard, she said, "If that's what you really feel you must do, your father and I will take her. We don't throw away family." I guess that brought me back to reality, and now it's twenty-two years later and I can't imagine life without my Jessica. My mom was the rock of our family. She lived for her family and I truly believe she gave me that strength even though I doubted myself many times.

It took me four years to stop mourning my mother and, as much as I miss her, I miss her even more for my girls. When Jessica graduated from preschool, all I could think was how proud she would be of my little peanut in her cap and gown strutting across that stage. The graduations, Melissa's wedding—she would have been so proud of all their accomplishments. Every day I find myself thinking and doing more things like my mother who, in retrospect, was indeed a wonderful mother who worked hard for her home and family. If I could be half the woman she was, I will have done well.

CHAPTER 11

"Always With Us, Watching Over My Children"

— as shared by Maryann Stech

Maryann Stech lives on Long Island and works as a secretary in a large public school district. She and her husband, Tom, have three children, the oldest of whom is a New York City police officer.

&

MY MOTHER, ROSE MCDONNELL, WAS A SWEET PEACEMAKER in the family. She was very easygoing and never interfered in our lives. When I had kids and stopped working, I did everything with her. We would go shopping and hang out together; we were almost like friends.

I moved to Virginia a year before she died, so I didn't see her that much. When she was in a coma and the doctors said the end was near, my sister said to come up right away. We were a six-hour drive away and my sister kept telling her that we were coming. She passed away quietly not long after we got to the hospital, with family members around her bed. I am sure that she waited until her whole family was with her.

When she died, I cried a lot. I remember her good qualities and am trying to be more like her. Whenever there were troubles with the kids or whenever something good happened, she was the first one I would call. Every time I am concerned about my kids, I pray to my mother and ask her to watch over them, to make it right.

My mother had a saying: "Love many, trust few. Always paddle your own canoe." She was always friendly and nice to everyone, but she impressed on us that you have to take care of yourself and not rely on other people. Love everyone, but don't be a follower. Think for yourself. Whenever I think about this saying, I feel like she's still here, still next to me, giving advice to me.

I feel like she's watching over my kids. She was very close to my children. The two older ones took her death very hard. I didn't know it but they both kept her Mass cards from the wake. Then, when my son Tommy was about twenty-one, he

Tommy Stech with grandparents, James and Rose McDonnell, at his confirmation.

was in a bad car accident. He was coming home alone late at night and another car cut him off. His car went into a telephone pole and knocked over a fire hydrant. Part of the pole snapped off, went through the sunroof and lodged there. It hit Tommy's head. At about 3:00 a.m. I heard a car horn blowing and a car pull into my driveway. I looked out the window and saw his car in the driveway with part of a pole sticking out of the sunroof. Then it drove away. All of us and our neighbors came out of our houses and my husband went after him. Tommy didn't realize what was happening; he was dazed and not making sense. The police came and sent him to the hospital. He had scratches and a slight concussion.

Later my husband and I passed the scene of the accident, where we saw the pole down and the fire hydrant knocked down. It was a terrible accident. The car was totaled and there was shattered glass all over it. I realized that Tommy could have died. The next morning we went to get the insurance card out of the car and, as we opened the door, we saw my mother's Mass card on the floor of the driver's side. I asked Tommy where it came from and he said that he always kept the Mass card attached to the visor. I hadn't known that, but I told him that he could have died and I thought my mother was with him.

Now that he is a New York City police officer, he keeps the Mass card in the flap inside his police cap, and that gives me comfort. I believe my mother is always with us, watching over my children.

CHAPTER 12

5:20 a.m.

— as shared by André De Shields

André De Shields has been an actor, director, writer, choreographer, composer, lyricist, and educator in a career that spans more than forty years. He has received numerous awards, including the 2009 National Black Theatre Festival Living Legend Award, the 2007 Classical Theatre of Harlem Award for Sustained Excellence in the Theatre, the 2007 Obie Award for Sustained Excellence of Performance, the 2001 Outer Critics Circle Award, and a 1982 Emmy Award, as well as several Tony Award and Drama Desk nominations. On Broadway, he played the title role in The Wiz *and performed in* Ain't Misbehavin',

André De Shields
[PHOTOGRAPH BY LIA CHANG.]

The Full Monty, *and the Duke Ellington musical* Play On! *In addition, he created, wrote, directed, and starred in* André De Shields's Harlem Nocturne. *He appeared in the film* Extreme Measures *with Hugh Grant and his eclectic performances on television include appearances on* Law and Order, Sex and the City, Cosby, Lipstick Jungle, Rescue Me, Life on Mars, *and* PBS Great Performances. *As Distinguished Visiting Professor, he has taught at Hunter College, New York University, Southern Methodist University, the University of Michigan at Ann Arbor, and Buffalo State College.*

ↅ

I HAD BEEN DREAM SLEEPING WITH EYES AJAR, sensing that at any moment the telephone might ring; and when it did, my soul ceased its dreaming, my heart stopped its beating, the clock persisted its ticking, but the Earth itself stood still. As if by magic the phone's handset was resting in my palm, and I placed it to my ear. In the seconds before Joanne spoke, something told me it was over. Something deep down at the very core of my being said, "John has died." And then Mother Joanne's calm but shattered voice echoed my soul's lament, "André, I'm calling to tell you that Johnny died at five this morning." It was only then that I focused on the face of the still chirping clock; it read 5:20 . . . tick-tock. John had been unique in my life. Never before had a man received my craving so deeply, so correctly.

The very first time I saw John he was not aware of me, but he must have felt the weight of my gaze upon his perfect self, for when he turned and our eyes met, I understood for the first time in my life the meaning of love at first sight. You see, in the anatomy of desire, the eyes are connected to the heart. I aimed my hot arrow of love directly at him, and John, thrusting out his chest, received it at the epicenter of his heart, and there it remained lodged until Sunday morning, June 17, 1995.

Five twenty a.m. has since become a special time of day for me; it is when I express gratitude to the Universe for having known a love as bottomless as the proverbial abyss. And I proudly wear the scars from John's burning kiss as a badge of courage, as a talisman of grace, for there is no more satisfying adventure than fiercely looking love in the face.

Do not mourn for those whom you have loved authentically and who have loved you in return. But do prepare—as if you were Saint Sebastian—to rejoice in the ecstasy and agony of the well-aimed arrow.

CHAPTER 13

Mother and Best Friend

— as shared by Lynda Johnson Robb

Lynda Johnson Robb is the elder daughter of President Lyndon Baines Johnson and Lady Bird Johnson. From 1969 to 1981 she was a contributing editor at Ladies Home Journal. *A self-proclaimed "professional volunteer," she was president of the National Home Library Foundation and chair of Reading is Fundamental, and serves on the board of directors of the LBJ Foundation and the Lady Bird Johnson Wildflower Center. She is married to former Virginia governor and two-term U.S. Senator Charles S. Robb.*

ຂວ

I HAVE SUCH HAPPY MEMORIES OF MY MOTHER. I keep up with all her friends and we share stories. I go to her Wildflower Center and partici-

Lady Bird Johnson on White House Lawn.
[COURTESY OF THE LBJ LIBRARY. PHOTO BY ROBERT KNUDSEN.]

pate in environmental projects carrying her message on. I love wearing her costume jewelry or a favorite dress of hers—even if it is short on me. My family looks through our photo albums and relives our adventures with Mother. I was very fortunate to have her as my best friend for so long. Recently we gave her scarves to some of her favorite friends so they could share her memory, too.

Left to right: Lynda Johnson Robb, Lady Bird Johnson, Luci Baines Johnson at the twenty-fifth anniversary of the inauguration of Lyndon B. Johnson.
[COURTESY OF THE LBJ LIBRARY. PHOTO BY FRANK WOLFE.]

CHAPTER 14

The Language of Music

— as shared by Dr. Yeou-Cheng Ma

Dr. Yeou-Cheng Ma is a physician and a musician, and the two people whose memories she keeps alive are her teacher and mentor. Her father, Hiao-Tsiun Ma, was her first music teacher and inculcated in Dr. Ma and her brother, famed cellist Yo-Yo Ma, the "language" of music. To carry on her father's legacy, Dr. Ma and her husband, Michael Dadap, restarted the Children's Orchestra Society (www.childrensorch.org) founded by her father. As a medical doctor and a mother, Dr. Ma regularly draws upon the inspiration of Dr. Mary Howell, who was dean of Harvard Medical School when Dr. Ma was a student there. Spurred on by the wishes of her father and her medical mentor, she writes frequently, including poetry that she has written in their memory.

ஐ

I REMEMBER MOST FONDLY THE TIME my father and I spent walking around the Jardin Luxembourg, when he explained to me how plants grew, and his telling me that the very first piece he conducted was Beethoven's Pastoral Symphony. So, as a toddler, I tried conducting the tall chestnut trees, singing the first phrase, and expecting them to

Yeou-Cheng Ma, Yo-Yo Ma, and Michael Dadap in concert.
[COURTESY OF YEOU-CHENG MA.]

continue the song, but they never did. We have pictures of me in the park with a violin case and a pull toy from the age of two and a half. He took me to lessons, sometimes by bus, sometimes by subway, and on occasion for long trips by train from France to Belgium.

He was patient, but he was also strict. One of my favorite stories about him was when he showed me the geranium plant we had on our windowsill. "See this plant?" he said. "It grows every day. If you do not grow and improve every day, you are less than a plant."

My father represented to me the quintessential teacher. I was home-schooled until the fifth grade in France. Therefore, he was not only my first music teacher, but also my kindergarten, first-grade, second-grade, third-grade, fourth-grade, and fifth-grade teacher. Because he was such an overwhelming influence in my developing years, I felt very close to him in thought as well as in philosophy. Many years later he had a long illness and was confined to his bed for three years after suffering a major stroke. We did not have long conversations during that period, but I felt that I could always go to him and ask him a question if I needed to. Even though he had a protracted illness, the finality of death was still shocking.

I think of my father whenever I think of music. I am convinced that music has been somehow programmed into my DNA. People often ask how I managed to work in medicine and music *and* be a wife and mother. For me, music is an integral part of my being—like breathing. No one asks how you find time to breathe.

My father was an accomplished scholar, musician, composer, conductor, and teacher. He conducted his life with utmost discipline, valued each moment of his time, and expected his students to do the same. He was a perfectionist and instilled in his students a hunger to learn and an untiring pursuit of excellence. He also encouraged children to learn to solve problems on their own and encouraged the development of their innate creativity.

My father always believed that music is a language and, therefore, something that children can learn from infancy if they are exposed to it—like a mother tongue. He founded the Children's Orchestra to help children grow in the language of music within a community that keeps the language alive. He always told stories as he was teaching, which is a fantastic way to connect to children, who love stories. Clarissa Pinkola Estes wrote, in *Women Who Run with the Wolves*, "Stories are vitamins for the soul, as pieces of pine pitch for fastening feathers to show the way." The work that [husband] Michael [Dadap] and I contribute to the Children's Orchestra brings music to the lives of young children at all levels of talent. The only requirement we have is for the child to demonstrate "fire in the belly" when it comes to learning and improving. We have now raised several generations of students and are pleased to see them succeed in their university studies, as well as in their professional and personal lives.

My father wanted to give the Children's Orchestra to my brother when he retired, but my brother was already quite busy with his performing career. So he turned to me and asked, "Daughter, would you like an orchestra?" I told him I would but that I couldn't do anything with it right then since I was starting my internship in pediatrics at Bellevue Hospital. But several years later—after I married, bought a house, and had a child—Michael confided to me that his life dream was to run a school for children to study music. This galvanized us in bravely "betting our mortgage" in 1984 to restart the orchestra with the last bit of savings that we had, which was twenty-five hundred dollars.

My father lived and breathed through music, as did my mother. He was the oldest of four siblings, all of whom he taught when he was a youngster and young adult. He had an insatiable need to educate and was undoubtedly delighted to have his own children to mold from the beginning. He had an incredible methodology which he applied to our early education. We were taught to be respectful and not get overly impressed by people's compliments. I recall an embarrassing moment when an adult praised my playing backstage after a performance and I modestly replied, "It's all in the method." He taught me a certain fearlessness and assured me and my brother that if something seems too difficult, just cut it in half, and if that is still daunting, cut it into quarters. Nevertheless, he was a strict teacher and somewhat intimidating. Occasionally, I would have a really off day, and my father would impatiently say, "I could teach a cow faster than I can teach you." And I had a small fantasy of how awkward the cow would be to maneuver in our very small apartment, and how much fun I could have if he spent time teaching the cow and I could run outside in the park. But were he a less strict teacher, we would not have been

Dr. H. T. Ma with children Yeou-Cheng and Yo-Yo Ma.
[COURTESY OF YEOU-CHENG MA.]

able to master the works that we did and might well have missed many opportunities, such as the great fortune to have been included in an all-star roster of artists who gathered together to raise money to build the Kennedy Center in Washington, D.C. It was on this occasion that we were introduced by Leonard Bernstein in a video clip that has recently aired on *Faces of America* on PBS. My father was terrifically protective of our time to study and practice and turned down many requests for us to perform. He firmly believed that youth should be spent in perfecting our craft.

The other person who remains such an important part of my life is Mary Howell, who interviewed me for medical school and was my dean and mentor for my first three years at Harvard Medical School. She was a role model for me in the way she cared for her patients and in the way that she raised her children. As the years went by, I discovered that she had been quite a serious musician and I reintroduced her to the world of chamber music. In her later years, she played chamber music almost every night!

Dr. Mary Howell
[COURTESY OF YEOU-CHENG MA.]

Mary had an incredible drive and energy. She was always advocating for healthy living, and for taking control of one's wellness. It came as a great surprise, and a painful one, when she opted for nontreatment and nondisclosure of her illness. From a mentor, she had become one of my best friends and I missed our conversations and the terrific times we spent with colleagues and friends. Her life was cut short by an illness for which she chose not to receive treatment, a decision that was difficult for her family and friends to accept. Losing a great teacher and friend on such short notice was a brutal shock to the system.

We took holistic health classes together, cooked food, and had great gatherings of people in her house, where people laughed and cried as they needed to and shared their lives with one another, drawing comfort from the support group that Mary fostered. She opened her house to people who needed advice and support. We had a great time playing chamber music with friends several times a year, including playing on the original instruments made by [anesthesiologist] Virginia Apgar on the occasion of the issuing of her commemorative stamp in 1994.

I keep her memory alive through writing, music, and teaching the principles that guided her life. I try to keep in touch with her children and keep them connected to the network of her loyal friends and associates. She donated her chamber music library to the Children's Orchestra Society, so our children keep her memory alive by continuing to play the music in the books that nurtured her soul during her latter years.

Remember the best moments you've spent with the person whose loss you mourn. Pass on the values, and how that person made you feel, to others, and to the next generation. Having a named scholarship in an institution of learning of significance to your dear one is one of the ways to propagate the memory of your loved one, and a way to pass on to posterity the stories of your loved ones, and to help young souls on their explorative journey to find their own voice.

Mary gave me an enormous gift by putting me in charge of the music for her memorial. I navigated the delicate task of choosing a quartet of her friends to play a contemplative piece and, in the spirit of inclusion, invited all of her chamber music friends, which I coordinated long distance during the month between her death and her memorial. I was fortunate that one of my colleagues and friends helped me by leading the violinists, and I led the violists in Bach's Brandenburg Concerto.

Mourning takes time. Be patient with yourself for a while. Then think of what your loved one would have you do. Some athletes have played games and competed in the Olympics very shortly after they lost a parent with the idea that their late parent would have wanted them to go on, however painful it may be.

I am by nature not a writer. I loved biochemistry in college but chose to major in chemistry instead because I had no desire to write a thesis. Mary Howell had been urging me to write ever since I started medical school and I absolutely shunned the idea. My father made it a point that we should chronicle our lives through diary writing, a task that was absolutely abhorrent to me, first because of my extreme need for solitude and privacy, and second because I had to write in Chinese, which was not my most fluent language. However, it greatly amused me to find out from a classmate at our twenty-fifth college reunion that she thought I took notes in Chinese in our physics class, whereas I was merely multitasking and trying to fulfill my daily quota of diary writing.

Yet, somehow, from the requirements of my high school that we write one poem a year, which was absolute torture for me because of my pitiful command of the English language, I learned a skill that was a lifesaver in times of stress and distress. [See Yeou-Cheng Ma's poems in appendix C.]

"The aim of life is to live"

— as shared by Ellen Gould

A native of Worcester, Massachusetts, and a graduate of Brandeis University, Ellen Gould is best known for her one-woman musical "Bubbe Meises, Bubbe Stories," which won two Emmy Awards for her work as both writer and performer. Gould has also had leading roles in productions from Lincoln Center to The Public Theatre and was featured in productions on HBO, PBS-TV, and NPR. Her other writing credits include "Confessions of a Reformed Romantic," "Seeing Stars," "The Glass House," and "Blessed is the Match," all of which received New York productions.

Ellen Gould

Gould lost two siblings at tragically early ages. Writing "Bubbe Meisses," a play that honors the memory of her two grandmothers, was also a healing process for her in dealing with the death of her nineteen-

year-old brother.

Gould received an MFA in Acting from NYU's Tisch School of the Arts and was the recipient of a Fulbright-Hayes fellowship in ethnomusicology. She is married to Daniel Ray, a market researcher and musician, and lives in New York City.

શ

My OLDER SISTER, PAULA, WAS KILLED in a car accident when she was seven. She was on her way home from Hebrew school, having just gotten off the school bus in a snowstorm. The driver that hit her never even saw her. I can only imagine the tragedy this was for my parents and grandparents. I remember her as a picture on the wall of my parents' bedroom—I was just two years old when she died.

My brother, Michael, was killed in a car accident when he was nineteen. I was twenty-three. He had been driving back from visiting our bubbe [grandmother] and zayde [grandfather] in Florida. It was a freak six-car collision on a North Carolina turnpike. A truck on the overpass above the highway broke through the guardrail and landed on his car. The loss of my brother was like an amputation with a phantom pain that was disabling.

I started writing *Bubbe Meises* in 1989, after my last bubbe died. Though the show was primarily about my two grandmothers, my brother was a sweet shadow hovering over the story. Michael had been killed in 1969. It took me twenty years to be able to write about it.

Bubbe Annie died at the age of ninety-three, having survived the loss of three of her grandchildren. (A young cousin was also in the car with my brother.) My first draft of *Bubbe Meises* was a kind of pastiche to honor Annie's memory because she was a frustrated vaudevillian . . . a pistol! Annie was still making dinners for the extended family at the age of ninety and holding court with her stories. Linda Selman, dramaturgy and acting coach, saw that draft and said, "There is something you want to say but this is not it." She encouraged me to think about an event that involved Annie, something that would trigger a deeper and more meaningful memory. As I searched for some moment of importance, my other grandmother, Bubbe Gittie, made her appearance in the story. I was suddenly transported to my bedroom, the morning of Michael's funeral. Bubbe Gittie was sleeping in the other twin bed in my room. (Unlike Annie, she was a widow and we didn't want her to be in her own apartment, alone, at a time like this.) It was early morning and I woke to find her sitting up on the edge of her bed, staring at the light pouring in the window. "It's so beautiful," I thought. "How dare it!" We sat in silence together, bound by grief, rage and wonder. "Yes, that's the story you need to write," Linda said, approvingly.

It felt dangerous to reenter that world of tragic memory. Every creative act, every healing act, is a risk, a leap of faith. Art only enables us to create light from the darkest places when we're willing to look hard into the darkness. I had needed the twenty-year separation to be able to take that look.

I got married in 1986, three years before beginning to write *Bubbe Meises*. I had terrible survivor guilt. The wedding was to be grand, redemptive . . . like a coronation. I thought I was eternal because I lost siblings so young and I was still here. You have a lot of guilt when you feel eternal.

I'm an agnostic, but as the marriage day drew closer I found myself screaming silently, again and again, to the God I didn't believe in. *How could you do this?* Then one morning I got an answer. It was Michael's voice in my head. "I'm OK, it's OK." It wasn't like the voice of a character wanting to write itself—I knew those voices. It was *his* voice that I heard, "It's fine. I'm fine. It's not what you think it is." "But if it's so 'fine' where you are," I found myself asking, "why don't we all just cut to the chase and go there?" Silence. "Damn," I thought. "I've scared it away, whatever, whomever it was." Then in a simple statement more worthy of Hemingway than my own lengthy lyrical expressions, the voice of my brother came again. "The aim of life is to live." Then it was gone—and with it my grief, at least that ragged, raging kind of grief. I had been given permission to live it all— the small, the grand, and everything in between. That simple statement marked the beginning of my long journey toward acceptance.

"The aim of life is to live."

Writing *Bubbe Meises* was a different kind of healing. Putting a frame around my story helped ease the terrible ache of powerlessness over death. I came to see how my private and necessary creative act could also help others with their grief and anger. To this day, whenever I perform the show, I make a ritual journey with the audience, through mourning to acceptance and, finally, affirmation.

There is no timetable for mourning—profound feelings of loss are always there, ready to be awakened. To some degree, mourning is a natural inhabitant of human consciousness. Mourning reminds us of our own impermanence. Was it Plato who said that death is so difficult that we need to meditate on it a little each day? The pain of impermanence goes hand in hand with the joy of living. It reminds us to take a chance, live and love fully, follow dreams wherever they take us. Or as Bubbe Annie sings, with pain and passion, after the loss of two of her grandchildren:

"Make waves, make love,
Make dinner,
And then sometimes just make do.
But take more out of life
Than it takes out of you!"

CHAPTER 16

A Poem, a Daisy, a Wedding Ring

— as shared by Jillian Levine

Jillian Levine lost her mother when she was twelve years old. She married her husband, Michael, on May 2, 2009, on the beach in Singer Island, Florida. When she was planning the wedding, she sought to find a way to include in the ceremony the wonderful memories she had of her mother. The poem that Levine ultimately wrote honored her mother in an upbeat way that reflected her mother's personality and added to the significance of her wedding day.

೮

Jill and her mother.

IT HAD BEEN WEIGHING on my mind how I was going to honor my mom on my wedding day. I looked for ideas on the Internet and discussed it with our rabbi, who was wonderful. Unfortunately, most of the ideas I came across I found very depressing. For example, leave an empty chair for the deceased person who is missing at the reception table, or bluntly acknowledge the person is missing during the ceremony, which felt more like a funeral. Other ideas included a memory table with photographs and that sort of thing. I really wanted to honor my mother in a lighter, happier way, as I know she would have been thrilled with Mike and the whole wedding day. I am fortunate in that despite how long she has been gone, I still think of her always and was old enough when she died to really remember her and the things she loved.

One night during one of my long after-work showers, where I always do my best thinking, I realized I had already been incorporating so many of these things into the wedding on her behalf, taking her favorite things into consideration as I planned my day. I realized that, to me, this is how I wanted to remember and honor my mother—by acknowledging, even though my family doesn't discuss it often, how much a part of our lives she still is.

I started thinking how it felt like my mom was everywhere in my life and part of my wedding day. She was the reason I had requested a single daisy (her favorite flower) in my bouquet, the reason we had yellow as one of the wedding colors (her favorite color). I used her wedding band during the ceremony. My mom always wore red nail polish (and so do I)—not very traditional for a wedding, but I loved the idea because those that remember her know she wore red. The list goes on and on. I wanted the family and friends who were attending our wedding to understand that, while I was of course missing my mom on my wedding day, she was still a part of it and that made me happy. To me, it was not a sad thing; I was surrounded by my wonderful friends and family and I was marrying the man of my dreams.

This is not the first event my mom has missed and it won't be the last. I wanted the way she was remembered and acknowledged on our day to have a happy tone, as she impacted so many lives and was always such a happy, fun, upbeat, and optimistic person. In the shower, I came up with the poem, and when I got out, I quickly jotted

Jill and Michael Levine on their wedding day.

it down. So that is how the poem came about!

In the end, I was so happy I included the poem. I think it worked out perfectly. It was a unique way of remembering her, which sort of fit the theme of our wedding: nontraditional. I think everyone was very happy I did it, and I did not get upset during the ceremony, which was my biggest fear in honoring my mom during the ceremony. It also made me really happy that everyone was so touched and I realized that I am not the only one who misses my mom every day. [See Jillian Levine's poem in appendix B.]

CHAPTER 17

Inspiring a Life in Song

— as shared by Tonia Tecce

Tonia Tecce is known as one of Philadelphia's favorite "popera" [a thematic and stylistic blend of operatic and pop music] artists. A mother of six and grandmother of twelve, she took off twenty-five years from singing to dedicate herself full time to her family. She returned to singing and began building a performing career in her forties, well past the age at which one even fantasizes about beginning a singing career.

Tecce has performed in Carnegie Hall and Philadelphia's Academy of Music and Kimmel Center for the Performing Arts, among

Tonia Tecce

other venues, and has recorded two CDs—What a Wonderful World *and*

*Smile. She stars in, and is the subject of, a one-woman show—A Cock-
eyed Optimist: Why We Believe, The Songs of Richard Rodgers—
written by award-winning director Michael Bush. While performing, she
often thinks of her father, who instilled in her a love of music and provided her with her first opportunities to perform.*

❧

M<small>Y FATHER WAS A DOCTOR.</small> He played the violin with his buddies
from medical school. One of them had a piano in his house. Daddy
would sit me on the lid of the upright and say, "Sing, Sissie, sing." I
couldn't have been more than four years old.

My father's office was on the side of our house. He always sched-
uled his most down-and-out patients at the very end of the day, knowing that they just might need a little cheering up. So after he treated
them, he brought them into our living room—still in his white doctor
coat—seated them on the sofa, called us girls downstairs, picked up his
violin, put his comb on the bridge of his violin because he said it made
it sound more like a Stradivarius, and accompanied us. My sister was
at the piano and I sang one song. Daddy knew the true healing power
of music. This didn't register with me until I was an adult, but I did
learn right away that I loved to perform.

I often think back to those days. It inspires me more to touch my
audience—to make them happy or make them sad, and hopefully to
make a difference. Every Christmas, every Thanksgiving, every holiday, we three performed for the family. There was a lesson to learn
there: the healing power of music.

Every Saturday afternoon my sister and I went to the movies and
saw Deanna Durbin and Jane Powell singing. After the movie, I sang
and danced down the main street of my town, all the way home. I
wanted to be just like the singers in the movie. At the age of eight, I
began singing on the stage with my sister at the piano. We performed
at Christmas parties, St. Patrick's Day celebrations, for Rotary Clubs
and Women's Clubs, and at every public event in our town and neigh-
boring towns.

My father never discouraged me from singing. As a doctor, he had
a very busy schedule. Whenever I performed in grammar school or

high school, he and my mother always came. He didn't want me to major in music.

At fifteen, I announced to my father that there was no need to think about college for me. I wanted to go right to New York after high school and sing on the Broadway stage. I was never very practical about things. My father said absolutely not, that I must go to college first and major in something other than music. It was important to have something to fall back on in case I didn't make it on the Broadway stage. I majored in sociology, which I loved, and continued to study voice, drama, and dance privately.

Daddy was being a very protective father. Later in life, after he'd had both legs amputated, he came to my concerts in a wheelchair. In some places, wheelchairs had to go in the back, but I insisted he be in the front of the concert hall—he was my father. After my performance, he would say that he hoped I understood why he didn't want me to go into a singing career back then, and he would cry. I told him that I understood and I had no regrets . . . and he should not either. He did what he did out of love, caring, and respect. And, I thanked him for that because I had the best of both worlds—a wonderful family and a singing career, even if it came to me later than I had planned.

I continued to perform extensively in college and took very important auditions. Exciting things were waiting for me after graduation. I had been accepted to sing leading roles in summer stock throughout New England and had performances in New York. In my senior year, I was heard singing by a talent scout from Paramount Studios, who asked me to come to California for a screen test. However, I fell in love and had to make a decision. I made the right choice. One week after graduation I was married and settled into my life as wife and eventually mother of six children. Naturally, my dreams of a performing career went out the window, but I never lost my desire to perform. That flame would never die.

When I was already past forty and my children were grown, I decided to find out if the voice was still there. I auditioned for and was accepted as a student of Juilliard Master Voice Teacher Florence Berggren, who subsequently referred me to Master Voice Coach Maestro

Martin Rich, conductor of the Metropolitan Opera. Immediately after I auditioned for him, I began working with Maestro Rich. In the years that followed, I made my New York recital debut in Carnegie Hall, sang in operas and recitals, performed with symphony and pops orchestras and, more recently, recorded two CDs. It took me a little longer than most, but I finally managed to turn my passion into a career.

My career is also a tribute to my mother, Jeanne Di Marino. She drove me many hours and many miles to voice lessons, dance lessons, and acting classes. My father worked long hours, so my mother did all that. I also think of my sister, who accompanied me at the piano, and my younger brother, who played the guitar. My mother died two years ago at the age of a hundred. She was still coming to my shows into her nineties.

She was also a remarkable woman. Not only did she raise us three children—she ran the practice for my father. They were partners, and together they dedicated their lives to my brother, my sister, and me.

My father received his education through scholarships. He loved to read and loved learning and made us read the classics. He was still taking classes at sixty. In his memory, our family established the Dr. Anthony J. Di Marino Memorial Library at Underwood Memorial Hospital in Woodbury, New Jersey, where he had served on the staff, and we purchased a life-size crucifix for the main altar in St. John's Catholic Church in Paulsboro, New Jersey, where we had lived and my father practiced medicine. When my mother died, we purchased a life-size statue of the Blessed Virgin Mary, and dedicated it, in her memory, to St. Patrick's Church in Woodbury, New Jersey, where she lived. Recently, in the church of Santo Giacomo Apostolo in the town of Torricella, Peligna, Italy, we dedicated the Blessed Virgin Mary's altar to both of our parents. Torricella is the town where my father's family—the Di Marino family—came from. The church had been bombed in the war and they are rebuilding it.

Losing my parents was very difficult. My mother lived twenty-six years after my father died. But they were more than just my father and mother—they had fifteen grandchildren. When my father played the violin, one of the children would come up and take the bow from him, place it on the strings and become so much a part of what Daddy was doing. He would work on projects with them—washing the car, cleaning out the garage, things like that. My parents were neither standoffish nor overbearing; they were just very involved in their children's lives, and that continued with their grandchildren. Nothing stood in my father's way. He said he'd rather live his life like a lion than a lamb. Even when he lost his legs, he never complained.

When you have much love and many profound memories of people, you cannot have only a little pain when you lose them. The depth of pain and suffering will be equal to the amount of love and memories you hold in your heart. You cannot know profound joy without knowing profound sorrow. We have to accept that. What do we do? In my opinion, we celebrate their lives. I celebrate my parents' lives by trying to emulate the goodness that they taught us. They taught us strength, endurance, and hard work, and gave us happy, happy memories. We must think about all they left us with, and we need to incorporate that into our lives. I find that the deeper you dig into your artistry, the happier you'll be. I am not able to sing and cry at the same time, so I leave all my pain and sorrow behind and I celebrate my God-given talent. Singing has been and continues to be my salvation. It's my strength. It allows me to forget about the "unhappy moments." Some people like to read, play cards, or do other things.

We have two choices: give in to our pain and suffering, or live how they showed us to live and love how they showed us to love. Do you hurt less? Do you cry less? No. But you set an example for your children and others. However, I will always continue to cherish and hold on to my memories and never let them go.

I carry my mother and father's prayer cards in my wallet. You take something that your hands can touch and keep it with you always. The newspaper that my father read the day he died, opened to the stock market page—I still have that. My mother had rosary beads. My father–in-law had a Tyrolean hat. Florence Berggren, my voice teacher, had a datebook into which she would enter her teaching schedule. Maestro Rich, my voice coach, had a lead pencil with which he entered our names in his datebook. I have all of them. My mother-in-law wanted me to have the grandfather's clock that had been in her house. I touch it every morning. I have photos of Ms. Berggren and Maestro Rich on my piano. When I practice and rehearse at home, I sing to photos of my mother, father, mother-in-law, and father-in-law that I have in my living room.

I believe that those whom we have loved and lost remain forever with us. It is this thought that gives me courage, strength, and resolve.

We can cry or we can make them proud of us. How would they want us to live our lives? By the examples that they set for us.

CHAPTER 18

A Living Memorial to
Victims of the Holocaust

— as shared by Boris Chartan

*B*orn in 1926 in the small town of *Podkamien in Eastern Poland, Boris Chartan is the founder and chairman emeritus of the Holocaust Memorial and Tolerance Center of Nassau County (New York) (www.holocaust-nassau.org). At the age of sixteen, Chartan was sent by the Nazis to a work camp, from which he and his father escaped eight months later. He and his parents spent the remainder of the war in hiding on a farm not far from Podkamien. After coming to America in 1946, he started a business and soon began to think about the importance of remembering the Holocaust and teaching future gen-*

Boris Chartan
GENE LESSERSON PHOTOGRAPHY.

erations about it. Working with the county executive, Chartan secured the funding and community support needed to build a Holocaust education center. The Holocaust Memorial and Tolerance Center of Nassau County, which is visited by some forty thousand young people from Long Island and New York City annually, is the only major Holocaust museum on Long Island.

৪০

WE KNEW OF THE NAZI INVASION of Czechoslovakia and Poland because a few people from there came to our town. The people who ran away from their homes came and told us what was happening. They told us about *Kristallnacht* and everything. A lot of people did not want to believe it.

I was fifteen when the Nazis arrived at the beginning of 1942. When they came in, we hid in a cellar under the house because there was resistance from the Polish Army and shelling in the city. We stayed in the cellar from 6:00 p.m. until nine in the morning.

The first morning of the occupation, the Nazis took my father and about fifteen other Jews to the big synagogue near our house and laid them on the ground with a Nazi standing over them with a gun. They let them all go in the evening. Three or four days later, on a Friday, they rounded up more Jews, those with beards—the rabbis and teachers. They burned down the five shuls [synagogues] in the town. My father did not have a beard and was not arrested. They put those they rounded up in barrels of cold water, beat them, and shot some of them; some they let go.

Standing from my house I could see the shul near our house burning in flames. In back of our house was the home of the number-two rabbi in the town. The Nazis found him right away and killed him. I ran into his house after he was killed and found it empty. I took his siddur [prayer book], which I still have. It is over a hundred years old. And I also took the Megillah of Esther. Today it is on display at the Holocaust Memorial and Tolerance Center in Glen Cove. The rabbi's two daughters survived. One moved to Israel and the other to Argentina. I had a cousin who survived and she was friendly with one of his daughters—the one in Israel. I told her I had her father's siddur and asked if she wanted it. She said no, that I should hold onto it. When the Nazis put my father and me in a work camp in Sasow, about four hours away by truck, I took the siddur and the Megillah with me.

My father had a dear friend, a Polish farmer named Marcianek. He and his wife had no children. She was a devout Catholic and went to church every Sunday. They lived about an hour-and-a-half walk away. They took my mother in with them.

One day, while cleaning the leader's house, my father was told that they were soon going to liquidate the camp and that my father should try to run away. A short time later—this was in the end of 1942—they took me to work and my father went with me to the mountains because they told him he was not needed in the house. As they marched us fifteen hundred Jews, there were big cornfields on the right and a tremendous forest on the left. After we had marched for one hour, they would have us sit down. It was getting dark. When they said the rest period was over, my father and I ran into the forest. They couldn't see us. I could hear my father running and he could hear me because the branches were dry and making noise. I yelled, "Tata, tata." We were five hundred feet apart.

We knew where my mother was because there was a Polish man who would smuggle in food to the camp and he told us she was with him. It took us two and a half days to get to her at the Marcianek farm. They hid us in a cave under the hay barn. You could lie or sit up in the cave, but you couldn't stand up. At night we went out to stretch our legs. The hole was covered with hay during the day.

Mrs. Marcianek used to go to church on Sundays, about thirty-five minutes away in Podkamien. On her way home one day, Ukrainians, who always fought with Polish people, shot her and many others in a ravine. Her husband knew of the attack and was afraid to go out and look, so, at about eleven that night, we went out and found a lot of bodies in the ravine. We found her, brought her to the farm in a wagon and, on Monday, built a casket and buried her—just the three of us—on the farm. Her husband left the farm and later remarried. My father used to send him packages; he died in the seventies.

We stayed in the cave until the Russians came in the spring of '44 and then we stayed on the farm. One day we decided to walk to Podkamien. There were no Jews there and so we decided not to stay. We followed the Russians—staying in the back of their lines—until we got to Dubno.

A lot of Jews had already come into Dubno and were staying in houses that were empty and had been owned by Jews. There was one shul they didn't destroy, so the Jews organized themselves. One rabbi, Moses Steinberg, survived the war with his wife and we made him the rabbi of the shul. Before the war, his brother had been the chief rabbi of Poland, but he was in Warsaw during the war and did not survive.

My parents and I lived in Dubno until 1945. Then we wanted to get to Germany because the United Nations Relief and Works Agency was very active there, setting up displaced persons camps. So we got on a truck to a suburb of Krakow and stayed there a little while. Then we boarded a train to Germany. They were freight trains—boxcars. The Americans were sending jeeps to the Russians and the boxcars were going back empty. We got on a train with a couple of hundred Jews and traveled through Czechoslovakia to reach Germany. We got as far as Pilsen on the border with Germany and Czechoslovakia when there was some confusion on the train and the Russians took us off and would not let us enter Germany. They put us in a camp in Pilsen until they finally cleared us and put us on a freight train to Munich with thousands of other Jews there. We stayed first at an army base in Munich and then were sent to a DP [displaced persons] camp. We were Orthodox and the camp had both kosher and nonkosher kitchens.

On July 15, 1946, my mother, father, and I got on a ship for America. The ship landed in New York and we moved into an apartment at Ninety-five Columbia Street on the Lower East Side. My first job was as a shipping clerk and later I was made a salesman with a button company owned by a German Jew. I spoke Yiddish, Polish, and some Russian, so I went right away to Washington Irving High School near Union Square and that's how I learned English. I went at night for three or four years.

We moved to Flatbush, Brooklyn, in 1949 and I married my wife, Renee, in 1951. We later moved to Long Island. In the early '60s I started to think about what *zachor* means—to remember—and how time was running out. When it was Kristallnacht and the anniversary of the Warsaw Ghetto uprising, there were anniversary programs and survivors who had watched it with their own eyes would speak about their experiences. But there was little else.

In 1977 I was president of the Plainview Jewish Center and thought that we should build a Holocaust remembrance inside the building. We kept getting older and older and I was afraid that people would forget about the whole thing. Some congregants who were born in America said it would be a terrible thing because how would it look when there was a wedding. I said we were not making a cemetery; we were making something that would be designed by an architect and would be beautiful and bring the Holocaust to the attention of the younger generation.

I had three kids—Steven, Michael, and Matthew. I had talked very little about the Holocaust, but when they saw me getting so involved, they supported me. It was completed in the late '70s. We had always said in the work camp and everyplace else that we shall never forget—that whoever survives should remember and never forget us. But after the war, we did not talk about it because we had to start a new life.

In 1986, I sold my building maintenance business. In that year, I also lost my oldest son, Steven. He was a dentist in Philadelphia and he was hit and killed by a car. That was the year I created a Yom Ha Shoah [Holocaust] observance at Nassau Community College with Irving Roth. We brought in Theodore Bikel and we had over fifteen-hundred Jews in attendance. It was the first major event of its kind in Nassau County.

When I was sixty years old, I started working in the Department of General Services. The Nassau County executive, Tom Gulotta, met with me one day and said he needed me to do outreach to the Jewish community. He said his father had highly recommended me. Six months later, I became assistant to the deputy commissioner of the Department of General Services.

At one point I brought Yitzhak Shamir, then the prime minister of Israel, to Nassau Community College. I was in charge of making all the arrangements. We had an escort of sixty motorcycles and twenty police cars—and mounted police around the college. When he arrived, Shamir, who knew me, said, "Hi, Boris—I don't get treated like this in Jerusalem." I replied, "Nothing is too good for you."

I told Tom that I would like to have a Holocaust education center in Nassau County because of the large Jewish community here. Tom immediately bought into it. I said we can't just make it Jewish, so we asked Rabbi Myron Fenster and Bishop John McGann to chair a Holocaust commission and we appointed commission members. When Albany failed to approve giving us two acres in Eisenhower Park, Tom said there was a two-hundred-and-four-acre park and mansion in Glen Cove and it would need only the approval of the county board of supervisors. But the building needed work. We had already raised thirty-seven thousand dollars and to put the building into shape would cost fifty-five thousand dollars. But we raised it quickly because there were enough people who believed in me. And, in September 1994, we opened after about two years of renovation. We also organized to have survivors go to schools to speak to the children about the Holocaust in their classrooms. And, we got a grant for buses to bring kids to the center.

My wife, Renee, died in 2009. We were married fifty-seven years.

In 2010, the museum reopened after an eighteen-month, three-million-dollar renovation. It is now an interactive, hi-tech center. One of the designers had worked on the Holocaust museum in Washington. We have a one-million-dollar operating budget and just received a grant to do renovation of the second floor to put in classrooms.

It's a living memory to my family. I lost about eighty or ninety uncles, grandparents, and other members of my family. And it is a learning center for kids. We want what happened during the Holocaust to be embedded in them so that they will go home and tell their parents—and someday their own children—what they saw and heard.

CHAPTER 19

Preserving Positive Memories Through Memorial Stones

— as shared by Susan C. Dessel

Susan C. Dessel, who holds an MFA in sculpture from Brooklyn College, created a series of memorial stones for deceased friends and family. She came to art late in life, having left corporate life in 1998. Her work for her BFA had to do with death and memory. The idea for memorial stones came from the Jewish practice of leaving stones on the graves of those visited in a cemetery. In her exhibit still lives, *she seeks to give identities to the women who arrived in New Amsterdam from Brazil in 1654 to help establish the first Jewish community in the New World. Dessel was able to discover through research the names of 215 of the women from the community founded by the 23 refugees (mostly women and children)* who arrived on the Saint Catherine, *each of whom was known on her tombstone only as someone's wife or daughter.*

Dessel at still lives *opening, 2009.*

യ

MEMORIAL STONES ARE BASED ON POSITIVE MEMORIES. When art is your work, what you do and how you do it really starts, I think, from the inside and comes out. Some of my work just comes from a year or two of thinking about images I constantly see around me. A lot of my work concerns death and the exploration of death and memory.

The stone I created for my mother is made of white earthenware. It is twelve by ten by five and sits on a shelf in my living room. It is a stone that represents the fact she had broad shoulders and I could lean on her. It also is a piece that represents her heart, and the top is glazed red because I always wanted to buy a black dress and my mother would say, "Don't you know that the girl in red has the most fun at the party?" I know that my sister can see my mother in it. My mother and all my aunts wore a perfume called Shalimar and it is a smell totally associated with my mother. The Shalimar bottle looks like strong shoulders. I didn't do it consciously but you can see it.

Another piece in memory of my mother has feathers dipped into cement. When dried, parts of the feathers stuck out and they moved, and to me that represented the life that exists after death. There are piles of fifty-two feathers, each one of them representing a week. My mother died in January 1973 and I had a pile for each year resting on

Dessel's Untitled (Remembrance No. 1).
[LENORE HOPP DESSEL.]

plain pine shelves . . . like a plain pine coffin. My mother had just turned forty-nine and this was for each year since she died. I did this in 2003, using mostly white feathers.

I made a piece called *Whose Counting*, in memory of members of the American military who died in Iraq. The wood I used was purpleheart. Each row represents a year since March 2003, and each bag represents a month and is filled with pebbles equaling the number of American military personnel killed in Iraq that month.

Dessel's Detail, Whose Counting, *2007.*

Another of my memorial stones was for a friend who was a journalist. He was chubby and so this is a round piece made out of white stoneware with an indentation in the middle and a black glaze representing the ink of a journalist. He died very young—of a heart attack in his forties. For me, my art is a way to communicate. If you knew him, you would recognize him in the piece because his form was very round and he was a warm and comforting person.

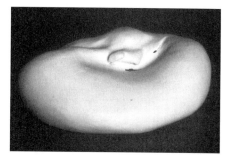

Dessel's Untitled (Remembrance No. 4), *2001.*
[JOJO LEWKOWICZ.]

The process is very important to me. As I work, I'm part of the process. Particularly with clay and the texture of the material, I feel that the material really does speak to me. There are parts of it that seem to form itself.

There were six women among the twenty-three Jews who came from Brazil and this exhibit [*still lives*] is based on the lives of the women and their female descendants buried in the Chatham Square Cemetery, one of three cemeteries in New York associated with the

Spanish and Portuguese Synagogue. There were no more cemeteries located in Manhattan because of health concerns. These women are part of our shared communal history.

Dessel Detail, still lives, *2009, TA0191.*
[PHOTOGRAPH BY THOMAS C. ANDRES.]

Dessel at Hunt's Bay Jewish Cemetery, 2008.

CHAPTER 20

Harnessing the Power of Grief

— as shared by Sherri Mandell

*S*herri Mandell is the mother of *Ya'acov (Koby) Mandell, who, along with a friend, Yosef Ish-Ran, was found brutally murdered on May 8, 2001, in the Gush Etzion community of Tekoa, five miles south of Jerusalem. Their bodies were discovered inside the Haritun Cave in Nahal Tekoa, fifty yards from Yosef's home. The killers, believed to be Arab terrorists, took rocks and bashed in the boys' skulls and then smeared their blood on the walls of the cave. No arrests were ever made. To overcome their own suffering, Sherri and her husband, Seth, created the Koby Mandell Foundation (www.kobymandell.org) to provide*

Koby Mandell
[COURTESY OF KOBY MANDELL FOUNDATION.]

healing programs for families struck by terrorism. Through the founda-
tion's programs—which include a camp for children of families struck by
terror, spiritual healing groups, and a Big Brother/Big Sister program—
the Mandells seek to help bereaved families become stronger by enabling
them to bridge their isolation and find meaning in their loss.

ℬ

He was only thirteen and was very smart. He loved to learn Torah and loved baseball and loved to be funny. He was very witty and was always telling jokes. He was very bossy. He knew a lot; he was very intelligent and I was waiting for one of his teachers to tell me he was a genius. When he was little and I would read him books, he would recite the words back to me.

Koby Mandell
[Courtesy of Koby Mandell Foundation.]

We really felt like his body was dead but we were going to keep his spirit alive and show our kids that you could keep on living. Because when they told us he was dead, I fell to the ground and looked at my husband and said, "What are we going to do?" Seth said we have three other kids and we're not going to let this destroy them. It was really him. And we wanted to do something that Koby would like.

Our children were invited to Camp Moshava in Indian Orchard, Pennsylvania, for three weeks. The kids had never gone to this camp before, but we were distraught and the kids were seeing their mother crying every day, so we thought it was a good idea for them to get away from us a little. We also went to America to stay with our families in the New York area, so we weren't so far away. We knew there was no getting away from it, but we were distraught and couldn't deal with the kids very well.

I saw that my kids didn't fit in. The counselor called and said my son was crying. My son said how he couldn't stop thinking about how much Koby would have liked the camp. He didn't unpack either. Now when I think about it, it was not a good idea to send them away. But we were desperate. I guess we thought . . . I don't know what we were thinking.

Then we came back and I spoke with Miriam Adahan, a writer and a psychologist. A week after Koby was killed I spoke with her and she said to do automatic writing. I'm left-handed and she told me to write with my right hand because it brings up your subconscious. And it uses a different part of your brain, I think. And she said to have a conversation with Koby. So I had this conversation and asked what we should do. He said to do something to make kids feel better. And then in parentheses I wrote "about themselves." Miriam Adahan brought me a journal to write in. My handwriting looked like his when I wrote with my right hand. (Koby was right-handed.)

During that year, our kids did get some help from psychologists but we felt like they needed to be where they could be understood, where they weren't so alone in this experience. And so we thought we would have a camp for twenty kids, but the intifada was terrible and so we had a camp for over a hundred children and we let them bring a cousin or friend that first year because nobody knew us and we saw how hard it was for our kids when they went to camp not knowing anybody. The camp was located in a kibbutz near Kiryat Gat. It was very powerful. We knew what we wanted to do. We had therapy for the kids. It was all indirect therapy—we had art therapy and drama that summer and one counselor for every three kids.

These were families who had suffered a loss—a father or mother, sister or brother was dead and they were sending their kids away to people they didn't even know. It took some recruiting. But by the second summer we had five hundred kids. The kids of anybody who had someone killed in the family could come. And we had a separate camp for about a hundred kids who were injured, and we had a retreat for ten families—about fifty people. And we had a two-day mothers' healing retreat that is now down to one day because of economics.

We did it because we wanted to do something for Koby and for our kids. We were like our own focus group of what was needed. Israel does not have anything for terror victims. Social Security came in initially and told us they would give us some money and then left us alone. They were not there for the families. There is a lot of attention in the first week and then everybody went away and we were left alone except for this wonderful community that stayed with us.

The camp created incredible happiness. This started seven years ago for kids eight to eighteen. A lot of kids have graduated. We now have the siblings who weren't there before, and now we take kids from accidents. And we have day camps for kids from Sderot [next to Gaza] who were traumatized [by the daily rocket fire], as well as disadvantaged kids from Dimona. We also now have American kids who train in workshops and then come to Camp Koby and work with bereaved children. That started three or four summers ago.

You always carry the pain with you; it's always going to be there. Grief is energy and power and you have to harness it. If you don't do something, it will destroy you. You have to find something within the love you have for a person to continue.

There is still power in the soul if you can tap into it—maybe not the soul but in the love you have for that person. And you can take that love and use it to create something from the destruction—just like Noah, who goes out after the destruction and creates.

It's a lot of fun and it brings tremendous happiness and it also brings honor to the people who have had losses. Most people think that after a year or two you are all better, but you need a lot of support. It's a very hard thing.

CHAPTER 21

A Book of Memories

— as shared by Janine Lavery

Janine Lavery is an elementary school principal who, as a teacher, created a photo memory book for her young children so that they would have a point of reference for recalling pleasant times with their grandfather. She later left the school district in which she was working to assume a position in the district where her father, "Coach" Bob Pratt, was a beloved teacher and coach.

৪৩

MY FATHER PASSED IN 1998 when my daughter Kirsten was five years old and my daughter Emma was one year old. I loved my father so much and he was such a strong presence in my life and the life of my family that I was afraid that my children would only remember the sense of loss because they were so young. I didn't want my kids to only remember what they did not have, but also what they did have.

At the time my father died, I was teaching third grade. I was working all day and my husband was back in school going into education after a career in business. I went to my dad's house as often as I could. I wanted to be with him, and it was difficult when I could not be with him. One night I could not go and tried to take my mind off not being there by going through pictures of my happy, healthy father. Five months before, the track team he coached had won the Suffolk County [New York] championship. It had been a wonderful season the spring before he died.

I decided I would make a memory book and so I selected photos of things the kids had done with my father—for example, Kirsten lying on the floor in his house while they were playing together. There was his big smile and her big smile. There was a photo of the Smithtown High School field that was dedicated in his name, and the girls were there for the dedication. But all the honors were not as important as the special time spent together. My father dressed up as Santa Claus every year and he put on a whole act and told a story.

My father died in May. We left the picture book out at the services and when family came to our home. This enabled Kirsten to share her memories, and it was cathartic for her. She would talk about the pictures, read the book and laugh. The book kept alive so many things that she would have lost. Both girls talk about these memories as if they recall them, particularly Emma, who was too young to remember but speaks as if she did.

The book served its purpose; it was created for the children but it helped all of us. It helped my mom focus, and it helped me to rise above my own grief. My father was only fifty-nine when he died, and he was always such a strong, healthy man. My mother was so grief-stricken, but she functioned when she was with my children. Kirsten would sit on her lap and they would talk. They remembered the happy times. They picked each other up.

I was so overwhelmed with grief but I decided it would be insulting to him if I didn't pick myself and my family up. My father told me that anyone could get hit by a bus and killed. "The only difference is that I know," he would tell me. My father was diagnosed when Kirsten was six months old, but he hosted the baptism at his house and didn't let anyone know until the day after.

He inspired people. That's why I wanted so badly to honor him. He faced his own mortality for five years. He never got to enjoy retirement. He instilled very strong confidence in me. It's easy for me to make decisions. He was a man of character, who instilled character in others. I knew from the start that I was not going to let our future be affected negatively by his death; he would have been disappointed.

At the moment of his death, one tear rolled down his face. It was the first time that I felt his overwhelming presence in me—I believe more than we understand.

My father is always with me; he's a part of me. What helps in living without his physical presence is that I believe the journey in life is so important that I feel he's on the ride with me. I don't know if it's his legacy or whether he can see, know, and rejoice in happy times. I know I call upon his example of strength in difficult times. I am a Protestant and was raised with Christian beliefs. I find great comfort in faith. I believe he's with me one way or the other. One time I was feeling very sad and almost felt my father physically hugging me. I felt my father's embrace.

One night, a few years ago, I took a back road to a board of education meeting. I had never gone that way before and I saw the field named after my father. The last time I had seen it from that angle was the day of the funeral, when the driver took us that way to show that the field was filled with flowers. I pulled over. I felt it was a sign from my father. *I'm here for you and I'm proud of what you have accomplished.*

CHAPTER 22

Comfort Through Community

— as shared by Leon Charney

Leon Charney is best known for his work in real estate and politics, but he is also a media personality, philanthropist, and cantor. In the 1960s, he became close to Israeli Prime Minister Golda Meir and worked with her to secure freedom for Soviet Jews. In the 1970s, he was instrumental in helping President Jimmy Carter bring together all parties to achieve the Camp David Accords.

Charney hosts a nationally syndicated TV show that deals with cultural topics, as well as political

Leon Charney with his mother.

issues ranging from what's going on in New York to the latest developments in the Middle East. He has written several books, including his best-seller The Mystery of the Kaddish: Its Profound Influence on Judaism, *published in 2006. In it, he examines the healing power of the prayer recited by a Jewish mourner following the death of a loved one and how, historically, Kaddish has helped to sustain the Jewish community in the face of tragedy.*

ॐ

W<small>HEN MY MOM DIED</small> IN 2004, I had an intellectual curiosity about why people said Kaddish. I am an Orthodox Jew and I know I am obligated to go to shul and say Kaddish three times a day. But nobody questioned why we do it and there seemed to be very little material on it. When I asked rabbis about who wrote this prayer and why do we recite it three times a day, I didn't get a complete answer. So I wrote the book and, to my surprise, so many people had the same

Leon's mother, Sara Ofshinsky.

thought—and obviously nobody had researched it. The book sold about twenty-two thousand copies between Israel, the United States, and Great Britain, and has been translated into Hebrew.

Saying Kaddish brought me a lot of solace. Because you can't say it alone, Kaddish brings the community together. And that was incongruous to me. Why do I need this *minyan* of ten Jewish adults? Why am I not able to say it by myself at home? The need to say it with a minyan was originally a custom and then it became *halakha* [Jewish law]. So you are not allowed—*halakhically* speaking—to say Kaddish without a minyan, and minyan means community. This, in my opinion, was the power of the rabbis—to keep the Jewish community together. When you are in a community, you form relationships because you meet every day and there is a collegiality and social aspect to it, as well as a psychological aspect. Most of the people saying Kaddish have the same psychological problems that you do; saying it is a kind of group therapy.

When someone dies, I think you need something to hold onto, to understand what the world and life are all about. The burial alone offers no sense of understanding of the world, but the Kaddish gives you a bridge or connection to some kind of value system. When you say Kaddish, the words have nothing to do with death; you are acknowledging the omnipotence of God. If you don't say Kaddish, it leaves you emptier than if you say it.

You can hire a proxy to say Kaddish for you as a way to alleviate guilt, but you delegitimize your own experience by paying for it. I suspect it began when people were traveling and couldn't say it and others then concocted other reasons. In Judaism, I think it's accepted as customary to hire a proxy, but Kaddish is meant to be an individual response. If you want to purchase it to alleviate guilt about not going to the synagogue, you'll have to come to grips with yourself to see if it's workable. And if you're not religious, why do you care about Kaddish at all? If you didn't think it was an integral prayer in Judaism, then you wouldn't feel obligated to say it. But there is no Jewish burial without the recitation of Kaddish.

Sephardic and Ashkenazic Jews have different customs and use different words in the Kaddish. Sephardic Jews don't say a form of the Kaddish on certain holidays. The Ashkenazi have a different way of saying it, but both need to have a minyan.

Saying Kaddish is a good response to bereavement because it's emotional. You're in mourning and you have an experience with a group in which people are observing the same ritual and it eases the pain. In some cases, I think people can commit themselves more to Judaism because they have gone through this year of Kaddish. What I saw happen is that you say Kaddish for eleven months and people go through a detox process—they don't want to stop. They are used to it and it gives them emotional support.

I met a guy saying Kaddish for his wife. You're supposed to say it for thirty days for a wife, but he didn't want to stop because it gave him a social and emotional experience. But in Judaism, you're not supposed to overmourn.

The Kaddish is made up of Talmudic passages combined with some Christian ritual. It came about around 1096 and it has no author. There were the Crusades, the killing of Jews, and black plagues and blood libels. Non-Jews, who were also losing people, had a place to go—church. A lot of people began moving to Christianity because they had no way to express their grief, and so the rabbis had to look at the laws of the gentiles to prevent the population from moving to Christian churches. So they democratized the Kaddish—they let everyone say it. Originally it was an elitist prayer for only the rabbis. Rabbi Akiva wrote *Kaddish d'rabonim*, which is said when you study Talmud. In it, you thank the rabbis for educating you. The rabbis took passages from the Talmud that affirmed that God is universal and cannot be questioned and that his judgments are always correct. It's an affirmation of God and therefore they don't talk about death—you just study and try to understand Judaism. That is what happened to me. Because of the death of my mother, I have read forty-five thousand pages of Jewish history and what I learned is that the function of a rabbi in today's society is to inspire you to study and not be the know-it-all. People find direction from learning, and Judaism is built on learning. We are told to teach our kids. If you get strident rabbis who try to tell you how to live, it is basically anti-Judaic.

Not everybody can give to charity [in the name of the deceased]. If you have the ability to give to charity and give them something in the name of the deceased person, you get fulfillment out of that. Charity is an excellent vehicle, but you need to go further. You can't buy everything in life. You need introspection about yourself and the world.

There's a difference between losing a child and losing a parent. If you lose someone not in the basic order of life, it is much tougher to overcome. You hear people say that not one day goes by that they don't remember their [deceased] child. When you lose parents, you don't hear that so much.

The Judaic process [of mourning] is quite interesting, with *shiva* [the seven-day mourning period following burial] and *shloshim* [the thirty-day mourning period following burial]. When you're sitting shiva, the third day is the most important because it is believed that, on that day, a person gets over the shock and can communicate with others and let them give him consolation.

I'm firm in my feeling that an unfortunate thing in life, such as the death of a parent, can catapult people into learning more about their religion.

You are supposed to say Kaddish in unison at the synagogue and not shout it out and then run out. You have to make it an internal experience in your life. If you are just mumbling words and running in and out, you don't get the same benefit. The fact that you're going to say Kaddish makes you feel good and the fact that you're studying makes you feel better.

Even nonreligious people go through extreme distress if they can't find a minyan. There is something very emotional about it. I've been in [real estate] closings where a person walks out for a minyan. Everybody stops so he can go and say Kaddish. The emotional impact of Kaddish is unbelievable and, God forbid, if you miss a day you feel tremendous guilt.

CHAPTER 23

A Search for Closure

— as shared by Leslie Rizzo

Currently working as a teaching assistant in an elementary school, Leslie Rizzo holds a degree in advertising art and design and still loves to draw and paint. She grew up on Long Island and lives in Centereach with her husband of thirty-five years. In 2005 their son Joe was working as an assistant district attorney in Suffolk Country when he died unexpectedly of complications from pneumonia. The twenty-five-thousand-dollar Joseph M. Rizzo Memorial Endowed Scholarship at the Hofstra University School of Law was established in perpetuity through the efforts of a former law school class-

Joseph M. Rizzo

mate and then colleague in the district attorney's office, Jessica Zimmerman. Despite his not having completed, at the time of his death, the paperwork required for admission to the bar, Joe Rizzo became the first-ever posthumous admission to the New York State Bar.

ℭ

WHEN JOE WAS EIGHT and making his First Communion, he came home from Catholic school and told me he had to do a reading. I didn't want to say, "You should be scared reading in front of all those people," so I just asked him if he was okay with it and he said he was. When he did his reading without a problem, I told his dad

Leslie Rizzo and son Joseph.

that one day Joe would be a lawyer. And that's the path he chose.

Joe at graduation with parents.

I have lots of good memories of Joe, but sometimes thinking about them is too painful. After his passing, I had a lot of trouble looking at pictures of him and I still do. A year after he passed, I had a breakdown and still go to therapy once a month.

Joe's doctor couldn't tell us about Joe's condition because of privacy laws. After Joe's death, I contacted a state senator to try to change that. To this day we still have no answers. We know what Joe died from, just not why he had to die.

The scholarship in Joe's name at Hofstra is almost complete. The scholarship was arranged by a Hofstra classmate and coworker of Joe's at the DA's office. She also had him inducted into the New York State Bar posthumously, at a ceremony in Brooklyn in 2006. These things have helped us in dealing with the death of our son. Joe's friend wanted to bring us some closure by doing this. I am so grateful to her for this wonderful tribute to our son. She is a true angel.

When I watch a television program about a parent who has lost a child, I'm looking for a reason to feel normal. To see a parent cry who has lost a child twenty or thirty years ago helps me to relate to them and understand that this feeling will never leave me—that it's okay to be sad or angry or to cry, whether it's one week, one year, or twenty years later.

I returned to work three weeks after Joe passed. My job saved me. I know that my close friends there tried to understand what I was going through but didn't have a clue. The only one who knows what you're going through is you and the only one who can get you through it is you.

Working kept my mind occupied. At home it was time to think about Joe again—to look at his room, to smell his pillow, to want him to come home more than anything. It took me over a year to start going through his things. I have kept all his law books, his personal collections of books, and books and more books. I felt like I was invading his privacy, but it had to be done. Some people leave a child's room the way they left it. For me, that wasn't going to work. To this day, I am still sorting through Joe's life. Some things make the cut, some I have to say goodbye to. I say goodbye every time I go through his things.

After Joe passed, someone gave me a journal to write in. And I thought to myself: *What am I going to do with this? Do I really want to read about how I felt when my son died?* For some reason I kept it and within a few months started writing down my feelings and thoughts. I don't write in it every day. Sometimes I write in it once a year. For some reason I am drawn to it, to get my feelings out. If I can ever help someone in the same situation, that would definitely be a comfort to me. [See Leslie Rizzo's poem in appendix D.]

The only advice I can give to a person who has lost a child is that it depends on the circumstances. By this I mean that if Joe had been sick and we had done everything to save him, I could have closure in knowing I did all I could to save my son, and had the time to say goodbye and I love you. If Joe had been in the military and died serving his country, I could have closure knowing he died doing what he wanted to do. If he was in an accident, you would still want to know why this happened to you . . . but the terms of how he died would be clear, and again you could have some closure. In our case, it's like a parent whose child is taken and you don't know where he is, and he is never found. You always have questions—no closure. Even the parent of a murdered child may find out who did it and can get answers at a trial. Why does a parent of a murdered child need to face their murderer? Why do they need to know every last detail of how their child died and what was done to them. Because they need closure . . . something I don't have and may never have.

About two weeks before Joe died, I remember looking out my kitchen door and seeing the most magnificent sunset I had ever seen. I recall saying to myself that I felt so blessed to have the family that I had. God blessed me with a wonderful husband and three wonderful sons. It couldn't get any better than that.

I feel fortunate for having had Joe in my life for the time I did. He taught me so much in the short time he was here. I'm a better person for having him as my son. And I, his dad, and his brothers miss him terribly.

Only a few weeks after Joe died, I had a dream about him. He was sitting right in front of me. All around us it was bright white. Joe looked thinner and healthier. I asked him if he could come home. "Mom, I can't," he replied. I felt my hand touch his face. It was so real I didn't want it to end. That was the last time I saw my son.

CHAPTER 24

Hard Work and Laughter

— as shared by Jack Klugman

Jack Klugman (who died on December 24, 2012) acted in movies and on television and Broadway in a career that spanned almost five decades. Among his many roles, he played a juror in the 1957 film Twelve Angry Men, *played the title role in the television series* Quincy, M.E. *(1977–83) and starred in the Broadway play* I'm Not Rappaport *(1987). He is, however, best known for his Emmy-winning portrayal of Oscar Madison in the television series* The Odd Couple

Tony Randall and Jack Klugman.

*(1970–75), in which he played opposite Tony Randall. Klugman, who was a longtime friend of Randall's, delivered the eulogy at Randall's funeral and wrote a book about their friendship—*Tony and Me: A Story of Friendship *(2005).*

ಸಿ

I DON'T BELIEVE HE'S DEAD. I love this guy. I knew him thirty years. We believed in the same thing. We both put in the work that was necessary to make it work and we were compatible that way.

He was really open to ideas. Comedy was wide open for him—anything could be funny. He never ever said no right away and he loved to laugh. Did he ever love to laugh.

When we went out on the road and he thought people were relaxing and not doing their job, he would run up and down and make them laugh and say, "Okay, now keep your mind on your work."

We had a wonderful personal relationship. We picked up after each other. When he died, it was like losing a father.

He married when he was in his seventies, which did surprise me. He called me and said, "You know, there is a big difference in age," and I said, "You love her—marry her." And they had ten wonderful years.

I remember his laughter. His laughter was infectious and he would laugh at certain things and you could do them over and over and he would laugh and have the best time. He would laugh so much.

I don't know if he's really left us with a legacy, but all I know is, I work very, very hard and conscientiously. Maybe that's the best advice: Go to work and don't look for personal glory.

To remember him, I just look at a picture. I have many, many pictures of Tony and me in the house and I look at them and remember where they were taken.

CHAPTER 25

Keeping Ancestors Alive

— as shared by Arthur Kurzweil

*A*rthur Kurzweil is perhaps the fore-most figure today in Jewish genealogi-cal research. His books on the subject include From Generation to Gener-ation: How to Trace Your Jewish Genealogy and Family History, The Encyclopedia of Jewish Gene-alogy *and* My Generations: A Course in Jewish Family History. *A frequent speaker on topics related to Jewish genealogy, he cofounded the first Jewish Genealogical Society in the 1970s. He is the author of* Kab-balah for Dummies *and* The Torah for Dummies. *As a publisher and editor—including editor-in-chief of the Jewish Book Club for seventeen years—he has commissioned and published more than seven hundred vol-*

Arthur Kurzweil in Hungary with cousin Zsura Barta.

umes of Jewish interest. Also an accomplished magician, he is a member of
the Society of American Magicians and the International Brotherhood of
Magicians.

೮

I'M NOT SURE HOW I FIRST GOT INTERESTED in genealogy. My father
was originally from Poland and liked telling stories. For years I grew
up on the stories of the little town where he grew up and it captured
my imagination. I got started listening to family stories and I learned
about my great-grandfather—the man I was named after. I found out a
lot about him and it made a difference to me.

For the people who can appreciate it, genealogy provides amazing
tools for exploring identity. I was named after my great-grandfather—
my father's grandfather. Many people told me about him; I found
wedding pictures and other pictures of him as a young man. I delivered a eulogy in the family last week and mentioned him because he
was the father-in-law of the woman who died and a couple of other
people were named after him. I described getting a copy of the death
certificate for my great-grandfather. It said he died in the synagogue
on *Pesach* [Passover]. When I asked my father he said he remembered
when it happened. I know the story and, for some reason, it is meaningful to me.

For Jewish genealogy nuts like me, paying a *shiva* [condolence]
call is a very lucrative endeavor because, when sitting shiva, often
photographs come out and stories are told about the deceased. We
don't study Torah but rather see death as an occasion to talk of the
deceased. It certainly is a genealogical activity. If you want to meet relatives, pay a shiva call and you will hear the old stories. They need
you and you need them. Some of my best friends are eighty-five years
old. When I was a young man, I was hanging around with them—seventy-five and eighty—and I needed them and believe they needed me
to need them. They were my translators of Hungarian and Polish. My
cousin in Warsaw used to write me in Polish and I had to find someone who could read Polish. I would see one of them on the street and
he would exclaim, "How come you haven't heard from your cousin?"

For me personally, my great grandfather is more real to me than you are. I certainly feel his presence. It says in the Talmud [rabbinic commentary and analysis of the Oral Law given to Moses on Mount Sinai] that your teacher is closer to you after death than during life. During life, he is in his place and you in yours, but when he's dead he is no longer restricted by geography. He can be with you all the time, and many people have found this to be true. The soul existed before this body and exists after this body and I have come to believe in these things, to know these things. I've spent more hours with my great grandfather than almost anybody. I grew up imagining about him . . . these are people who are alive.

I saw a wedding that Rabbi [Adin] Steinsaltz performed and the first thing he did was to invite the ancestors—by name—to come under the *chupah* [wedding canopy]. Genealogy changed my life. I started in the early '70s when I was in my early twenties and somehow it grew. It started in a big way when I found a book in the Forty-second Street Library. It was a Yizkor book [a memorial book about a town in Europe destroyed by the Nazis] from my father's town, Dobromil—a *shtetl* [small town in pre-Holocaust Eastern Europe with a largely Jewish population]. The town was once part of Austria, then Poland, then Russia, and now Ukraine. A *landmanschaft* [Jewish Benevolent Organization for immigrants coming from the same locale] put together a Yizkor book, and two pictures of my great grandfather were in that book. I said to myself: There must be more! I was going to do Jewish genealogy.

I have been doing this for forty years and I've given about a thousand lectures over the years. Some people love genealogy and some don't. Also, I interviewed many [Holocaust] survivors and, in a strange way, sometimes those who had the worst experience came out of the Holocaust with faith, and some who did not have as bad an experience lost faith and became angry with God. Why are some turned on by genealogy and others are not? Some people don't want Yom HaShoah [Holocaust Remembrance Day]. For me, I remember the names of those who were killed—one hundred three Kurzweils who were killed. Somehow it makes a difference.

When I was the VP and editor of Jason Aaronson Publishers, a young editorial assistant told me that she had learned her mother was a child survivor and her grandparents had been killed in the Holocaust. Her grandmother had been shot on the street in Lyon and her grandfather taken away. Nobody knew what happened to him.

I went home and went through the lists published by the Nazi hunters Serge and Beate Klarsfeld as a memorial to the deportation of the Jews from France—thousands of names of people who were on trains to the death camps. I find indicated on a certain train transport that her grandfather died on the train, and the next day I bring the book to the office and show it to her and make copies. The next day her mother calls me and tells me that the book, and the information, brought her some comfort because all her life she wondered what nightmare her father underwent and now knowing he died on the train gave her closure.

The Nazis give us numbers and the Jewish genealogists take away numbers and give us names.

I love going to cemeteries; it's a very live place. The reason there are words on the stone is that the stone hopes someone will come along and read it. I went to Poland for seven weeks and all I did was read the stones and see the family groups. There is a lot of life in those cemeteries and it brought me to an eternal present. These loved ones are as alive as my memory allows them to be.

There's a woman I've been counseling who lost her mother a number of years ago and was still very upset. I showed her the Jewish text that says if you don't stop mourning after eleven months, God will often give you something else to mourn about. Sooner or later you say there is a time to stop mourning. The body dies and the soul goes on and we have to let the souls go on. We can't hold them back; this is what life is about. It sounds very harsh, but there is a time to mourn and cry and weep and be brokenhearted.

Galway Kinnell wrote a poem called "Wait," in which the writer is talking to someone about to commit suicide—someone who lost a loved one and is despondent. There is a line in the poem that is extraordinary: "[T]he need / for the new love is faithfulness to the old." So if you lose your partner and want to re-partner, don't feel it is not being faithful to the one who died. The old love caused a space in you and it is a space that wants to be filled. It's such a beautiful idea—the person who lost a wife or husband says I have to be faithful to the one who died, and that in finding someone new you *are* being faithful.

CHAPTER 26

"A Small Step"

— as shared by Stan Gadiel

Stan Gadiel met Charles "Chick" Senico while sharing family beach umbrellas at a swim club. When the conversation turned to golf, Senico persuaded Gadiel to clean off his clubs and come out to play the game he had played only briefly fifteen years earlier. The two became very good friends and played in the same foursome for eight years, until Senico's death from lymphoma at age forty. In his memory, Gadiel has sponsored and organized an annual golf outing for the past twenty-four years, the proceeds from which are donated to the American Cancer Society.

I COULD TELL FROM THE BEGINNING that Chick had a wry sense of humor that fit right in with mine. A few months before his death, he got wind of a surprise birthday party being thrown in his honor. So when everyone yells "Surprise," he opens his shirt and reveals a hand-lettered message to the group that says, "I can't believe it"—only in slightly more colorful language—and then pulls out a small camera and starts taking pictures of everyone taking pictures of him. You had to be there—it was pretty funny.

Chick was a friend to me and my family. He was also my younger son's godfather. We knew he was on limited time after he started the chemotherapy, so we were somewhat "conditioned" to the final outcome. But death is never easy to take, especially for someone so young. I was the executor of the estate and was therefore constantly reminded of his passing. It's difficult, twenty-four years later, to remember exactly how I felt in those early days and months after he died, but I think I was still in a bit of denial that it happened at all. This was the first passing of a contemporary of mine and, as most people, I think I was unprepared to emotionally accept it even though intellectually I knew what had happened.

He was always "up" and brought happiness when you were around him. He always loved to golf even though he rarely could break ninety. Since his death, we've conducted an annual golf tournament to raise money for the American Cancer Society. The outing is relatively low-key—blue-collar-like—which is the way Chick was . . . a very down-to-earth person.

Every year at the outing I say, "Maybe this money will help someone else *not* die of cancer so young." I feel that I'm doing something right—something that might make a difference. Not a big difference, but a small step toward possible major and positive differences. I interact with Chick's two boys, who are thirty-eight and forty-one now, and I feel good that they're doing well. Even though I think about Chick occasionally anyway, this outing helps to bring back some of the good times that we had. There are also a number of participants in the outing that knew Chick, and we sometimes tell golf "war stories," especially from the numerous Myrtle Beach trips we took.

It's hard to watch someone dying from a debilitating disease, knowing that they're now on borrowed time, but that's not the picture you want to remember. I guess it's almost trite to say, "Remember the good times," but that's what I do. Think about the jokes and laughter that you shared. Think about how much the person meant to you and your family but focus on the positive. Doing that should lead to fonder memories and maybe ease the immediate feelings of grief.

CHAPTER 27

A Recipe for Remembering

— as shared by Florie Wachtenheim

Florie Wachtenheim lives in Westchester County, New York, with her husband. They have three grown sons. Among her many community activities, she served as president of her local public school board of education.

૪૭

M<small>Y MOTHER WAS EIGHTY-SEVEN</small> years old when she died. She built her life around very fundamental concepts and values, with family and the well-being of those she loved being most overriding. For

Florie and her mother,
Ann Hammelburger.

as long as I can remember, she maintained an impeccable home, prepared meals for the family, and was very devoted to the well-being of each member of our family.

I am most likely to think of her before and during the Jewish holidays. My mother had the family to her house *erev* (the eve of) Rosh Hashanah every year. The last time she had us all, she was already very sick. It was very challenging for her, and the memory of that night and the effort she put into it is something I'll never forget.

Cooking is an interest my mother and I shared. Having come from Europe, my mother was quite good at all the most traditional dishes—homemade gefilte fish, for example. That is probably the single tradition that I carry on and that means the most to me. She is in my head and in my heart when I compose each holiday menu. Either consciously or subconsciously, I tend to include one of her recipes at each holiday meal. She is there with me when I'm considering what to make, when I'm preparing it, when I put it out, and when I enjoy the look on someone's face as they think about "Maw Maw" when they realize that what's on the table is a dish she used to make. [See Florie Wachtenheim's recipes in appendix E.]

Mourning is a process that I believe should be indulged. I had a very difficult first year; I let myself feel the grief and I didn't hide it from others, and I think this helped move me along. A few weeks before my mother passed away, though we had not been able to have an authentic conversation about her imminent death, she said to me, "I had a hard time saying that my mother died, but it got easier." That was the extent of our conversation, but, as I think about it now, she knew that our pain would be enormous, and the grieving would be intense. But she also knew that there would be a process and that it was okay to start feeling better at some point. And that's how it happened, and I'm glad she understands.

CHAPTER 28

The Gift of Unconditional Love

— as shared by Jodi Kerper

Jodi Kerper lives on Long Island, with her husband, Michael, and their two children. She is a past PTA president and chaired Arts in Education for thirteen years. In her roles as wife, mother, and friend, her mother remains her greatest inspiration.

ช

ACUTE MYELOGENOUS LEUKEMIA— powerful words that I learned at the age of fifteen. Words were powerful to my mother. My mother loved to read and write, and she wanted to be an English professor. Her educational dreams were sidetracked when she got married and had her first child before she received her bachelor's degree.

Jodi Kerper's mother, Gail Gorin.

Words were powerful to my mother. Education even more so. After having three more children she decided to go back to school to earn her degree. I remember my bedtime stories being Romeo and Juliet during her Shakespeare class and the poetry of Shelley and Byron while she studied poetry. I remember her pulling all-nighters at her typewriter to finish her term papers.

Her dream was sidetracked a second time and never realized because she died from acute myelogenous leukemia at the age of forty-one, just two classes shy of the elusive bachelor's degree. It was November of 1983 and I was a first-semester freshman at college. I was left to grieve and push forward day after day, redefining myself as a motherless daughter. The girls on my dormitory floor in college would talk to their mothers on the phone once a week. Sometimes they would complain about their mothers. What I would have done to have their problems on that day.

Those girls, who considered themselves young women, had no idea how powerful a word can be. The word "mother." How all of us have taken that word for granted, and those of us who know that wish we hadn't. The power given to us by our mothers. The power we wasted and lost.

Time passes and you mature. I got married (without her) and had my children (without her). People are resilient, we adjust and we rationalize. And we do the one thing that she asked of us: to live our lives, because life is for the living.

Time marches forward and you wake up one day and realize that you can remember her with a smile instead of a tear. I try to keep her memory alive by sharing her brief life with my children. She would have had six grandchildren. I could just hear her reading them stories; I can see her editing their college essays. Empowering another generation with the words she loved so much.

As the twentieth anniversary of my mother's death approached, my husband, Michael, came to me with an idea. He had started running and biking for charity and, ironically, did a lot of fundraising for the Leukemia and Lymphoma Society. He asked me if I wanted to organize a run on Thanksgiving morning to honor my mother. The money raised would go to the Leukemia and Lymphoma Society. I thought about the opportunity to share her story . . . her legacy. Perhaps her story can continue to be written.

The rest, as they say, is history. We just held the eighth annual Gail Gorin Memorial Turkey Trot. We greet over fifteen hundred runners on Thanksgiving morning. We smile and feed them breakfast and check them in for a chip-timed race to benefit the society. Our friends and family come out to run and support the event. We have even met some of my mother's former classmates from elementary school. But mostly we are in a sea of strangers, putting one foot in front of the other, raising one dollar at a time so that one day no girl will have to say goodbye to her mother because she died from leukemia.

Our hope is that someday no daughter will become prematurely motherless—that whether that mother loves words or sports or any other avocation, she will always be there with the most powerful words for her children: unconditional true love.

CHAPTER 29

A Grandmother's Wisdom

— as shared by Hazel Dukes

Hazel Dukes became well known in the 1960s and 1970s as a civil rights activist and has remained an outspoken champion of social justice for minorities and the poor. She was president of the Great Neck-Manhasset-Port Washington-Roslyn NAACP branch on Long Island (today called the North Shore branch) and, in 1989, became national president. For the past sixteen years, she has been president of the New York State NAACP. She has received numerous awards, including, in 2009, African-American soror-

Three generations: Hazel Dukes with grandmother Sarah Hopson, and mother, Alice Dukes.

ity Delta Sigma Theta's highest award for social action in recognition of her involvement with the NAACP.

ଚ

MY MOTHER'S MOTHER WAS SARAH HOPSON. My mother had a sister who died at an early age, so my mother was raised as an only child. She and her mother were very close, and after my grandfather died my grandmother moved in with us. We had never really lived too far apart.

We lived on Mason Street in Montgomery, Alabama. My grandmother moved in with us in the 1950s and she died about ten years later when she was in her seventies. I was in my twenties.

My grandmother was a very strong woman and her dress was impeccable. She did not like to see women not dressed appropriately and she passed that along to my mother and me. Her hair was always immaculate and washed and groomed—she had to be well groomed. So if you were going out to church, you wore clothes considered appropriate for church. If you were going to a dance, your clothes had to be appropriate for that. My grandmother had a choice of clothes for every occasion.

Those are some of the values and traditions I now keep that I associate with my grandmother and mother. In addition, I was taught to try to complete everything I get involved with. And I was taught to make sure the choices I made are valuable choices—nothing frivolous. As a result, I don't get involved in idle talk about things that have no meaning or consequence. The things I get involved with have outcomes—someone has benefited from something I did, such as when I work with young people.

I've been a member of Delta Sigma Theta, an African-American sorority, since college. It will be celebrating its one-hundredth anniversary next year. We are all professional women who work in many areas of human and civil rights. We also have at the NAACP a youth and college chapter, and I also belong to The Links, Incorporated, which works with young people.

These are the things that keep my grandmother's memory alive because they are what I saw her doing. She was always busy with something that had results—not just busy work but constructive work. She was a homemaker and a church missionary. She made sure that anyone at the church who was sick had food, and she accompanied church members who were sick to the doctor. The things I do today were instilled in me by my parents and grandmother.

I got involved with the NAACP over thirty years ago. An uncle of mine had been very involved locally in the NAACP. I saw what it was about and it caught my attention. When I got involved, my grandmother thought it was great.

Because my grandmother didn't believe in frivolous things, she was very active. She didn't like the thought of people sitting around and doing nothing. She believed that those who were not involved in their community were wasting their time. She would say that she was so busy that she didn't have time to die. I've used that expression myself; it keeps you grounded and moving.

I remember another of her sayings. It was a funny one: A dog that brings a bone will carry a bone. It means that if people tell you something and you respond, they will go and tell somebody else. But if you don't respond, it will die. She didn't make it up. It was a saying in our culture that she liked to use.

I think that children who have not had a chance to be mentored or had a relationship with their grandparents have missed out on an important part of their lives. To have grandparents involved in their learning and growing up is important for the development of young people. Yes, parents are very important but grandparents have the wisdom.

CHAPTER 30

Honoring the Founders of Jewish Savannah

— as shared by Marion Abrahams Levy Mendel

*M*arion *Abrahams Levy Mendel was born in 1917 in Savannah, Georgia, where she has lived her entire life. She has been a docent of the Judaica Museum at Savannah's Mickve Israel Congregation, which receives about eight thousand visitors each year. She has served on numerous boards, including the Bethesda Women's Board, the Widows' Society Board, the Savannah Chapter of the American Red Cross (of which she*

Marion Abrahams Levy Mendel and daughter, Joan Levy.
[PHOTOGRAPH BY GARY LEVY.]

later became president) and the Sisterhood of Temple Mickve Israel (of which she also became president), and was the first female member of the Board of Congregation Mickve Israel.

Mendel is a direct descendant of Benjamin Sheftall, one of the original Jewish settlers in Savannah and author of the Sheftall Diaries, *which pro-*

*vides a detailed account of Savannah's Jewish community between 1733
and 1808. The Torah that came with her family from London to Savannah in 1733 is still read during Mickve Israel's Sabbath service each July to
commemorate the founding of the congregation in that year.*

೭ು

My FATHER WAS A DESCENDANT of Benjamin Sheftall, one of the
original forty-one Jewish settlers who arrived in Savannah in 1733.
My mother's family, the Guckenheimers, came here in the 1850s in
that great wave of German immigration. My father's most famous
ancestor was Mordecai Sheftall, the highest-ranking Jewish officer in
the American Revolution and benefactor of the Jewish community.
My mother's grandfather was Simon Guckenheimer. He owned a
large wholesale grocery business and was chairman of the Building
Committee when the present Mickve Israel Temple was built. Both
families have been active and prominent in the civic and political life
of Savannah down through the years.

One of my earliest recollections from when I was a very small girl
was of watching my father, Edmund H. Abrahams, go into his "den"
after supper. In that room stood the antique mahogany desk composed of numerous drawers and cubbyholes containing countless letters, documents, scraps of paper, envelopes with interesting stamps,
old currency scrapbooks, prayer books—you name it. Seated in front
of the old desk, Daddy would pull out a drawer, take from it a letter,
carefully unfold it, read it, fold it back and return it to its envelope (if
it had one), and repeat the process with another letter or paper. As I
grew older, occasionally he would invite me to come over and look at
what he had been reading and I would diffidently do so, but, for the
most part, I couldn't have been less interested. What a lost opportunity! Many times since, I have regretted those times!

It wasn't until I married B.H. Levy and moved back to Savannah
after B.H.'s stint in World War II and started looking through the
desk again that I really became conscious of what a treasure trove we
had. B.H. had been a history major at the University of Virginia—a
real student—and he became interested in my family's history in early

Savannah.

Looking back, I realize I led what is termed a "privileged life." I was an only child, probably spoiled by my mother's siblings as well as my father's. I attended a private school because Savannah's schools, then as now, were not very good and my parents wanted me to be prepared to get into a really good college. (I eventually ended up at Smith College.) I took dancing lessons, piano lessons, and riding lessons. I attended religious school at Temple Mickve Israel and was confirmed there in a class of twelve, most of whom had started out with me in kindergarten at private school but, in the intervening years, had switched over to public school, as I had much later than most. I attended temple services with my grandmother in her Guckenheimer family pew most Saturday mornings, thereby forming a habit of years. I was a charter member of the Winnie Davis Chapter of the Children of the American Revolution, sponsored by the Daughters of the Revolution, the Savannah chapter of which I am now the oldest living member. And, of course, I was a Girl Scout—my mother, Mildred Guckenheimer, having been one of the first Girl Scout Leaders.

In 1933, the year I was sixteen, I marched in a parade celebrating Savannah's bicentennial. The line of march was composed of groups from various social and ethnic groups in the city. Our group was made up of individuals from our temple in colonial dress. The main speaker of the day was our president, Franklin D. Roosevelt. What a thrill to stand out in the middle of the stadium and look up behind home plate and watch him speak!

My mother's family, the Guckenheimers, lived in a modest frame house on Whitaker Street facing Forsyth Park. There lived my grandparents, my mother's younger siblings, and a series of registered nurses who, from time to time, attended my grandmother, whose health required frequent surgeries from which she always seemed to be recovering. There was nothing I liked better than to spend an afternoon with that rambunctious brood! My uncle Sims played the ukulele, my grandmother Fanny played the piano (when she was well enough to come downstairs), and we would all join in singing and having a rare good time. My uncle Sims and my aunt Jean taught me the popular songs of the day and the dances to go with them, delighting especially in coaching me with the most risqué lyrics of all. Of course, at the time I was no more than six or eight years old and had no idea what I was singing.

B.H.'s family, the Levys, came to Savannah at approximately the same time as the Guckenheimers, only they came from Alsace (which at the time was under German rule)—a little town called Trimbach. We visited there in 1962 with our children. The cousins still live in nearby Strasbourg and we keep in touch with them, visiting back and forth occasionally, especially the branch who have since moved to Paris.

My husband was frequently asked to address small groups on the subject of the history of the early Jewish community. I accompanied him to those lectures, bringing along a sampling of some of the smaller objects inherited from my family, the Sheftalls, and including Sheftall Sheftall's cocked hat. B.H. was a trustee of the Mordecai Sheftall Cemetery Trust, which administers the old cemetery given to the Jewish community by Mordecai Sheftall. There had been no burials there since 1897 and it had fallen into considerable disrepair. The trustees were making an effort to identify graves and mark them properly and B.H. set about research on many of its occupants. This ultimately resulted in the first of B.H.'s books.

Mickve Israel's museum depicts the congregation's history from its founding in 1733—just five months after the Colony of Georgia was founded—to the present. The museum had its beginning as a small alcove at the eastern end of the Mordecai Sheftall Memorial No. 2. It was merely two glass-topped cases containing not much of historical interest—the old Sunday School organ, a few old prayer books, and later the portable Ark containing the Torah that the Jewish settlers brought with them from London to Savannah in 1733.

Every life has its share of "woulda, coulda, shoulda" and mine is no exception. Looking back over my long and happy life, I often regret that I have not been more proactive, but that's just not my style. I'm exceedingly proud of my heritage and the part my forebears have played in the history of this beautiful city in which we have been blessed to live. It is a family tradition that continues through my children's involvement in the synagogue and their devotion to the museum. Both my son B.H., Jr., and his wife, Margie, a transplant from Jacksonville, Florida, have served active terms as *parnas* (what we call the president of our Temple Board—a remnant of our Sephardic heritage). My daughter Joan Levy presently serves as a member of the board. It is my fervent hope that someday at least one of my four grandchild chicks will return to the roost in Savannah and carry on the family heritage of religious and civic participation in its life.

Marion Abrahams Levy Mendel and daughter, Joan Levy,
in Temple Mickve Israel Museum.

CHAPTER 31

Reliving TV's Golden Age

— as shared by Leona Schwartz

Leona Schwartz is the daughter of actor Eli Mintz, who portrayed Uncle David on The Goldbergs *television series during the Golden Age of Television. Since 2009 she has been sharing with audiences her insights into* The Goldbergs, *including little-known facts about its creator and star, Gertrude Berg, and her father's personal story. Schwartz is currently a recreation therapist for the frail elderly and a choral director for the Sweet Adelines in*

Leona and her parents.

Holtsville, Long Island. She is married with two grown children.

ଚର

*T*HE GOLDBERGS WAS TELEVISED LIVE from New York when it went on the air in 1949. It was done live until about 1953 and went off the air in 1956. After *The Goldbergs*, my father did a lot of Broadway and off-Broadway. He was in *Jimmy Shine*, the musical with Dustin Hoffman, and I remember meeting Dustin Hoffman.

My father's given name was Edward Satz and he changed it to Eli Mintz. He was the seventh of ten children. His first job, at the age of seven, was as a busboy in a brothel. During that time he also had some acting jobs in the Yiddish theater in Lvov. At the age of ten he was already playing roles of old men.

My father came to the United States by himself in 1927 at the age of twenty-three. Two of his older brothers were in New York: Alex, with whom he had a close relationship, and Ludwig, who was a well-known actor. If not for Alex, I think Ludwig might have tried to get my father deported because he didn't want the competition. And he didn't like the fact my father was here illegally. Many years later, my father became a naturalized citizen.

In 1947, the actress Gertrude Berg, who had had a long-running radio program called *The Goldbergs*, approached Menashe Skolnik, who played the role of Uncle David on the radio, to reprise his role in the Broadway show she was planning called *Me and Molly*. He said he couldn't because he had other commitments and he recommended my father, whom he knew from the Yiddish theater. They were both short and spoke with a nasal quality. Berg gave him the visual once-over and had him say a few words and just said, "Yes." She was a really astute person.

One of the most interesting aspects of his career is that he was able to create the physical appearance of Uncle David—the walk and the talk and the dress and the make-up. The costume department had bought a suit for him from Brooks Brothers. He wore it for opening night, but he went to the Bowery to buy a second-hand suit that he felt was more appropriate for this character. That is the suit that remained for the Broadway run—and that is what the character became.

He played the role not only for the Broadway run—it ran for about a year—but also on television. My father got the TV role over about thirty other actors who had auditioned for it. And he remained in the role from 1949 through its television run that ended in 1956—with some hiatuses, which were common in those days as a result of sponsorships or contractual nonrenewals from one thirteen-week period to another. He also played the role in the 1950 movie adaptation of the television series.

In 1973, there was a Broadway musical based on *The Goldbergs* that starred Kaye Ballard. My father was the only original member of the television cast to appear in the show, which was called *Molly*. He also did countless appearances on television programs, such as *Playhouse 90*, *Kraft Theater*, *Dr. Kildare*, *Ben Casey*, and *United States Steel Hour*. These were both dramatic and character roles. He also did commercials. One—for Alka Seltzer—was quite memorable for the line, "Try it, you'll like it." My father played the role of a waiter who was standing in the background when the line was said.

His last movie was *Stardust Memories* in 1980. He died at the age of eighty-three in 1988.

A documentary about Gertrude Berg, called *Yoo-Hoo, Mrs. Goldberg*, came out in 2009. I had met the filmmaker, Aviva Kempner, while I was visiting a Jewish museum in the city. They were having a symposium that day about *The Goldbergs* and she had her film crew in the lobby interviewing people about their memories of the show. When we walked in, a woman was talking to the crew about her memories of Uncle David. When she finished, my husband, Allen, asked the woman, "Would you like to meet Uncle David's daughter?" She said yes and he went to get me. The filmmaker heard this and interviewed me in the lobby. She subsequently contacted me and asked to interview me again. We spent many hours together, and there is a short segment of me in the movie.

As a result of the film, the filmmaker was asked to speak at many of the film's openings. She invited me to the Lincoln Plaza premiere and she subsequently put the art theaters on Long Island that were showing it in touch with me. I spoke at the Cinema Arts Theatre in Huntington and the house was packed; it was unbelievably emotional for me. When you think of how long ago the show went off the air and they were showing it in 2009 and the theater was packed with about four hundred people—they even held it over for an extra run because of its popularity. People had amazing memories. I was also approached by an organization about speaking at greater length about my father's life. So I created a forty-five-minute talk, followed by a showing of an original episode, including commercials. I also offer a Q&A at the end, which often results in interesting inquiries from the audience. I use a DVD of the show, but I also own ten episodes on sixteen-millimeter film which were given to my father.

My father talked about a number of the things I include in my talk, but I also did a lot of research with my mother. My mother—she used her maiden name professionally, Hasha Saks—and I had done a program on my father and *The Goldbergs* for the Jewish Historical Society of Greater Bridgeport in Connecticut. My mother, who died in 2008, would have liked to do the interview for the film *Yoo-Hoo, Mrs. Goldberg*, but it would have been arduous to get her to Washington, where the interviews were being done. She was disappointed she couldn't do it. They were married forty-four years when he died.

My father was a self-made man and was largely self-taught. Learning was important to him. He had jackets with patch pockets, which gave him the flexibility to carry things—a paperback book, a paperback dictionary and a newspaper. He had a tremendous command of English and was always well spoken. People he met in his professional travels thought he was a well-educated man and were impressed with him because of his English. And they were impressed with his fountain of knowledge. My father could quote the Torah and philosophers, and he knew the works of a lot of Yiddish writers, whom he also could quote. He was rather poetic himself and would occasionally write poems for my mother, and always with a little bit of humor in them.

I admired him and I am very bookish myself and enjoy reading. We used to read together—it was a family activity. We'd pass the book around and read to each other. I think it made me interested in books and speaking and mastering the English language as well. My mother's background and education were very different from my father's; she was college-educated, through to the master's level. Like my father, she spoke very well. The combination of the two of them influenced me.

I also learned from him integrity. He always treated people fairly, even though he was not always treated fairly himself. But he didn't become jaded. To make ends meet while he was in *The Goldbergs*, he would go to the mountains and work some of the smaller hotels. They'd book him for three shows a night and pay him two hundred fifty dollars when it should have been at least five hundred dollars. He gave at least one-hour, one-man shows that included monologues in Yiddish and English, very funny stories, Sholom Aleichem stories and characterizations.

He was always studying people, and what better place to study people than the automat. He would look at people there and try to conjure up what kind of a life they had. I find myself doing it. He did it to find characterizations that he would portray—stealing from real life. He would steal a look or a walk or a cough. He had a whole monologue about coughing and it was absolutely hysterical.

I always try to be fair with people, not misrepresent myself, and try to follow through with what I promised. My father ingrained that in me. And I'm also very interested in people, which is something else he taught me. Sometimes I'm there just to listen and sometimes I help out with advice. My father would speak with someone for fifteen minutes and find out that person's life story. He approached them in a nonthreatening way and they felt he wanted to know without prying and without judgment.

And of course I get my love of the arts from my parents. My mother loved music—she was a gifted concert-level pianist and music educator. My father loved the theater.

In his heart my father strongly believed in God but did not go to temple because he couldn't afford it. That, combined with the fact he worked so many weekends in the Catskills.

One of the things my father used to quote to me was the line, "To my own self be true." He usually said it when he was dissatisfied with something I had or had not done. I was a very obedient child and when he would essentially accuse me by saying that, I was very hurt and offended. Philosophically, if you are not true to yourself, you are not true to anything or anybody. You must do things in the most honest way you can. I think a lot about that and have quoted it to my own two children.

Leona, her parents, and sister.

CHAPTER 32

Babe Ruth: "The Name is Magic"

— as shared by Linda Ruth Tosetti

Linda Ruth Tosetti is the grand-daughter of New York Yankee slug-ger George Herman "Babe" Ruth, the so-called "Sultan of Swat," who set numerous records during his playing career (1914–35). His mark of 714 career home runs stood for almost forty years, and his 1927 single-season record of sixty home runs was not surpassed until 1961, when the season was extended for the first time.

After learning that many books about her grandfather had numer-ous inaccuracies and failed to men-tion his humanitarian work, Tosetti teamed up with filmmaker Byron Hunter to make a documen-

Linda Ruth Tosetti
[COURTESY OF LINDA RUTH TOSETTI.]

tary—entitled "Universal Babe"—to bring public attention to that work. She also has developed a talk about her grandfather that she delivers to audiences throughout the country. In addition, she has created a website (www.thetruebaberuth.com). A homemaker who was born in 1954, Tosetti lives in Durham, Connecticut, with her husband, Andrew, whom she married in 1980.

ↄ

For MANY YEARS, I accompanied my mother, Dorothy Helen Ruth, to Cooperstown, New York, for the annual Hall of Fame baseball induction. She was invited as the only biological daughter of Yankee great Babe Ruth.

Five years after her death in 1989, I suddenly received an invitation to attend. I really didn't expect it—I'm just the granddaughter. But I remember my mom saying, "Pay attention, you're next." My mom must have set it up before she died because she didn't want Babe to be forgotten.

When my husband, Andrew, and I went to the Hall of Fame, I recall standing in the middle of Main Street when a man who remembered seeing me from a prior induction ceremony walked up and asked me to sign a baseball for him. He handed it to me and said, "Nice to see Ruth in town again." So I said sure and signed "Linda Tosetti." The man said, "No, I want to see Ruth." So then I signed "Linda Ruth Tosetti."

Anybody signing a baseball on Main Street in Cooperstown is going to attract attention and, before you knew it, they were twenty deep all around me, handing me baseballs to sign. It was like a mob and it scared the living hell out of me. My husband was asking, "What the heck is going on here?"

No one from the family had been at the induction ceremony for the previous five years, and stores in town stopped carrying small things with Ruth on it to sign. But after I started attending the ceremonies, the stores began carrying pictures of Babe again, as well as dolls and plaques—all kinds of things. So Babe was back in town and now I understood what my mother told me: "If you're not there,

Babe's not there. If you *are* there, Babe will be there."

The year 2014 will mark the one hundredth anniversary of Babe entering major league baseball and I plan to attend [the ceremony at Cooperstown]. I'm hoping they will show the documentary on my grandfather, "Universal Babe." The documentary was my idea and it tells the untold story of Babe as a humanitarian and his work on behalf of minorities. At a time when segregation was the norm, my grandfather made a powerful statement about racism by participating in exhibition games with African-American players. He also actively assisted the Women's Softball League at a time when women in baseball were disparaged.

In December 1942 he signed an ad with forty-nine other German-Americans denouncing the Nazi persecution of Jews. The full-page ad appeared in ten newspapers, including the *New York Times*, at a time when this issue was not being talked about. I didn't learn about the ad until a few years ago when someone sent me an article about it. In fact, I didn't find out who my grandfather was until I was in the eighth grade and a classmate asked, "Is your grandfather Babe Ruth?"

I said, "Yes, why?"

He said, "Do you know what he did?"

I said, "Yes, he played ball for a living."

He said, "Yeah, but . . . ," and then began to fill me in on how my grandfather was the home run king and the greatest ballplayer in the world and was really famous.

So when I came home for lunch, I said to my mother, "You didn't tell me that I was famous."

She said, "Because you're not."

I said, "Your father was famous, you're famous and that makes me famous."

She said, "No, it doesn't; you didn't hit the ball."

Until then, she never really talked about him. The Lindbergh kidnapping in 1932 affected my mother greatly and she didn't want people to know who we were. But now that the cat was out of the bag, she answered my questions about my grandfather. But her tone of voice always said, *Don't think you are better than anyone else because you're not.* She told me, "There are people who are better than you and worse than you—don't forget it."

At the time I learned my grandfather was famous, I was just getting over a crush on Davy Jones of the Monkees. We had no baseball in the house. We did not follow it on TV or radio. We were four girls and two boys and none of us played baseball. I remember once being picked for a game and throwing to the wrong base.

So I picked up some books my mother had in the house to read about my grandfather, and my mother would correct what was in the books. I didn't know then to go to newspaper articles. All I had were books and they were wrong, so my mother became the one who gave me information about my grandfather.

We had pictures of Babe in the house, but they were pictures of him with the other players. My mom, however, had a couple of pictures she loved that showed her as a child with him. And one of my sisters has a picture he gave to my mother for us kids. It is a picture of him on which he wrote, "To my grandchildren. Sincerely, Babe Ruth."

When I saw it, I said to my mom, "Sincerely?" She said, "Yes, that's how he signed." I haven't seen a picture or a card on which he wrote "love." As far as I know, he never wrote "love" on anything. My mom said she once got a ten-dollar gold piece from him for Christmas and he just wrote on the card, "Pop."

I found that the writers of these books about my grandfather knew about him signing the Holocaust ad and about his playing with the Negro leagues, but none wrote about it. All they wrote about was his drinking and carousing. But a lot of it wasn't true. My mother said he wouldn't have been able to pick up a bat if he had had as many women as the books reported. It was said that he had a cigar every time he had a conquest.

He had ADHD (Attention Deficit Hyperactivity Disorder) and only slept two hours a night. When he couldn't sleep, he would go to a train yard and watch the trains come in. He had a lot of extra energy and that is why he broke curfew. In 1929 they tested him and found that he had to eat six times a day to fuel himself for the energy he expended. So he had a voracious appetite since childhood, but you would never see him falling down drunk like he was depicted in a movie. His drink of choice was beer.

There are so many things I want to straighten out about my grandfather, but you can't do much in a two-hour documentary or any movie. For instance, Babe didn't die of throat cancer that they say he contracted because of his lifestyle of smoking cigarettes and drinking. He died of nasal pharyngeal carcinoma, which is a genetic cancer commonly found in Asian people. Thank God, as a family we are safe. My grandfather did not smoke cigarettes. He said that it steals your wind.

But we decided to center the documentary on the two things people don't know about Babe that demonstrate his humanitarian side—Babe and the Negro leagues and the Holocaust.

Alas, few books mention my grandmother.

While Babe was married to his first wife, Helen, he had an affair with my grandmother, Juanita Jennings. She was a society girl from San Francisco whom he probably met while barnstorming. They got together in 1920 and my mom was born February 2, 1921, in New York City.

After my mother was born, Babe wanted to marry Juanita but she said no. The baby was premature—weighing barely five pounds—and had rickets. So Babe brought the infant to Helen. Helen said she wanted to raise the baby, having wanted a baby so badly but not being able to have one. Helen told Babe, "She belongs to you—I want her." Juanita was happy with that decision. Helen and Babe separated in 1926, and Helen raised my mother until she [Helen] was killed in a fire in 1929, when my mother was seven years old. Three months later, Babe married a showgirl named Claire Hodgson, who had a child, Julia, from a previous marriage. Babe adopted Julia, and Claire adopted my mother.

My mother later married Daniel Sullivan and had three children. Then she married my father, Dominick Pirone, and had three more children. I was born in 1954 and am the youngest of her six children. I like to say that I'm Babe's babe's babe.

Mom (Dorothy) with her dad (Babe Ruth).
[PHOTO COURTESY OF LINDA RUTH TOSETTI.]

Mom (Dorothy) playing cards with her dad (Babe Ruth).
[PHOTO COURTESY OF LINDA RUTH TOSETTI.]

Mom (Dorothy) with her dad (Babe Ruth).
[PHOTO COURTESY OF LINDA RUTH TOSETTI.]

Over the years, Juanita and her husband, Charles Ellias, stayed in contact with my mother and she called them "Mumsie" and "Popsie." I think she suspected Juanita was her mother and not Helen. She knew that in her will, Helen had left my mother twenty-five thousand dollars and she described my mother as "my ward," not "my daughter."

And Juanita would say, "That Linda has the color of my eyes—green." I also look like my grandfather. People who knew my grandfather have said they can't believe how much I am like him. They say I look like him, laugh like him, and scrunch up my nose like him. He died in 1948 and when I hear this, it's like a connection for me—and I'm tickled pink.

When Juanita was dying in 1980, she told my mother that she was her mother. My mother said, "I kind of thought so, but why didn't you tell me before this?" She said, "Babe was supposed to have written a letter telling you. I thought you knew all these years and just didn't want to discuss it. You treated me like your mother, so I thought you knew."

My mother would visit Babe when he went to the barbershop—he would have a shave and a trim every day. It was convenient for her to see him there, and she would bring my older brothers and sisters and they would climb all over him while he was getting a haircut.

I put all these pieces together after my mom died. She told me a lot of it. And I have been going out and speaking to groups about my grandfather.

There is a connection between us that I can't put a label on. I have inherited the energy of the man. My mother understood and saw that energy. She told me that when Babe would visit hospitals, he would ask to see the sickest children. He would just stick his head in a ward and children there walked who were not supposed to walk. Others who had not been able to sit up would sit up. My mother said it was remarkable.

He was aware of the energy he had—and it is still around. When my mother and I used to travel, people would be as happy as all get-out to see us. It was beyond me. The name Ruth would cause people to smile. The energy of the man is still making people happy. It is otherworldly. My husband has seen it many times. I always welcome it. More and more people keep telling me they love the Babe. It never gets old. My mother once told me "the name is magic," and I believe it.

Appendix A

Here Comes My Mother

Meryl Ain, one of the authors of this book, wrote the first two poems below. The first, in honor of her mother, was written during the last weeks of her mother's life. The second poem, in memory of her grandfather, was written eight years after he died.

Meryl Ain with mother, Helen Fischman.

ଽ

DURING THE LAST TWO WEEKS when it was clear that my mother was not going to survive her bout with the aggressive cancer that was ravaging her body, but not her spirit, I tried to find a way to capture her essence in a way that would comfort me after she was gone. My mother was like the human embodiment of sunshine and always loved sun and fresh air, so I decided that whenever the sun shone brightly I would think of her.

In addition, since the Beatles' song "Here Comes the Sun" was already one of my favorites, I would make it my mother's anthem. At my son Daniel's wedding, which took place less than two years after she died, I even chose it for our mother-son dance. During our dance, Daniel gave me a big hug and said, "She's here." Whenever I hear the song, its uplifting tone energizes me and I think of my mother.

I wrote the poem "Here Comes My Mother" in the two weeks before she died. It was inspired by "Here Comes the Sun." I read it to my mother on her deathbed and she gave me a big hug and told me she loved it. But as I said at her funeral when I read it again, my mother loved everything that I did. Such was my mother, and one of many reasons described in the poem why she was such a powerful force in my life, and will live forever in my heart.

HERE COMES MY MOTHER

Here Comes the Sun
Absolutely
My Favorite Song
Lilting hopeful anthem
No one describes it
Better than the Beatles.

Here Comes My Mother
Definitely
My Best Friend
Sunny Soothing Confidante
No one radiates optimism
Better than My Mother.

Here Comes My Mother
Cheerfully enlisting to serve
Her country, her family, her friends

With words and wisdom and devotion
Armed with needle and thread
And quiche and brownies and toys.

Here Comes My Mother
Bringing order out of chaos
Joyfully doing my laundry
Gladly setting my table
Happily organizing my closets
Smilingly straightening my counter.

Here Comes My Mother
Reflectively listening to every dilemma
Positively spinning every disaster
With a Solution to Every Problem
Casting light on the open window
Obscured beyond the closed door.

Here Comes My Mother
Dazzling with Pride for her Family
Singing Happy Birthday
Framing business cards; applauding speeches
Celebrating prose, praising poetry
Nourishing and encouraging children of all ages.

Here Comes My Mother
Resplendent with Dignity
Alight with Affection
Glowing with Grace
Clothed in Kindness
Sparkling with Support and Selflessness.

Here Comes the Sun
Here Comes My Mother
Giving life, warmth, light,

Illumination, sustenance,
Comfort and consolation
Shining Eternal Presence.

Here Comes the Sun
Here Comes My Mother
Bright and Radiant Source
Everlasting Luminous Force
The Sun is forever
And so is a mother's love.

Grandpa Harris Trachtenberg with Arthur and Meryl.

MY GRANDFATHER HARRIS TRACHTENBERG died when I was twelve. Throughout our childhood, he was a consistent nurturing and attentive companion to my brother and me during our weekly visits as well as the summer our family spent at the beach with him and our grandmother Mary. He played all kinds of games with us and also had us emulate the quiz games of the era. Although he did not have the benefit of higher education himself, he was a strong believer in life-long learning. He had us memorize the capitals of every state in the

United States, all of the presidents and vice presidents, and the most difficult spelling words. He then tested us on the assigned topics the following week. For every correct answer, he would reward us with pocket change. As the retired owner of a drug store with a soda fountain, he would take us to the local soda fountain and order cherry sodas for us. The taste of cherry soda still brings back sweet memories of my grandfather.

Following his death, my grandmother came to live with us and lived in my parents' home for eighteen years, where she took up painting, enlarged her social circle, attended our weddings, saw two great-grandchildren and lived to almost ninety. But the loss of my grandfather when I was at such an impressionable age left a huge void, which lasted for many years. When I was a college student, I decided to go to the cemetery by myself to visit his grave in an effort to make meaning out of this loss. Following that experience, I penned the poem below. Surprisingly, the philosophy still makes sense to me.

To Grandpa

Oh paint me a sea
Of cherry soda
Beneath a sky
Of cotton candy
Sun and sand and cool salt water
The summer I was seven
I swam with Grandpa every day
The summer I was seven
And I lost my breath
As we ran a race
Along the golden shore.

Oh build me a mountain
Of virgin snow
Beneath a sky
Of icy diamonds

Snowmen and snowballs and blizzards and snowfalls
The winter I was seven
Grandpa and I shoveled snow
The winter I was seven
But I caught many colds
And had to stay inside
Sometimes when it snowed.

Oh sing me a song
Of Happy Birthday
Candy, games
And chocolate cake
Confections spun for me by Grandpa
The spring that I was nine
We took many walks in the country
The spring that I was nine
But I had to walk a little slowly
Because Grandpa needed a cane
To get around with then.

Let's play a game
Of Ghost or Rummy
Learn a lesson
In spelling or nature
Grandpa taught me many things
The autumn I was nine
I could spell the hardest words
The autumn I was nine
But he sat much more in his chair
And played games to hide the pain
That I didn't want to see.

Oh play me a dirge
Of reality
The pain of becoming

The pain of ending
My body changed and puzzled me
The winter I was eleven
New powers blooming, old powers fading
The winter I was eleven
Grandpa could no longer walk
He needed his wheelchair to get around
And found it difficult to speak.

Oh I hear the drums
Of death and decay
Right beyond the song
Of growth and strength
I came into my own; I lost my love
The summer I was twelve
The miracle of life, the joke of death
The summer I was twelve
I sang in vain to drown out the moans
And then ran back for one last look
At all I ever knew or loved.

Oh what do I know
Of anything?
Of reasons for living
Excuses for dying
The mystery is greater than before
Now that I am twenty
I see that nothing remains the same
Now that I am twenty
Winter, summer, fall and spring
All stay awhile, then pass away
Leaving their marks in one way or another.

Oh what can I say
With certainty?

Of the meaning of cycles
Of the pattern of life
I cannot know; I can only feel
Now that I am twenty
Truth eludes me more than before
Now that I am twenty
I see only that we each have our season
Some leaving more spring behind
For those who must face the winter.

Everywhere

Jillian Levine wished to include her mother, whom she lost at age twelve, in her wedding ceremony in some meaningful way. In her remembrance, she tells of the thought process that led to her use of certain cherished objects and choice of colors on her wedding day, and her inspiration to write and recite a poem that captured her mother's upbeat and optimistic nature. As she relates:

 හ

I CAME UP WITH THE POEM IN THE SHOWER, and when I got out I quickly jotted it down. In the end, I was so happy I included it. It was a unique way of remembering her, which sort of fit the theme of our wedding: nontraditional.

EVERYWHERE

You are everywhere
You are the daisy in my bouquet
You are the ring on my finger
You are the yellow in the flowers

And the red on my finger nails

You are the sun in our wedding theme

You were my strength in planning this wedding

You are the picture that I carry with me in my bouquet

You will be the image dancing in my head when the DJ plays the song "Shout" later tonight

You have become a part of each one of us

You may not be here, but today and always, I feel you everywhere

"We invite the soul of all who are deceased—a generation has gone but their light forever brightens the land."

Blank Space

In her remembrance, Yeou-Cheng Ma describes in detail the powerful influence that her father, Hiao-Tsiun Ma, and her mentor, Mary Howell, had on her personal and professional life, and how she perpetuates their memories. Although English was not her first language, both encouraged her to write, and one of the ways she honors their memories is through her original poetry.

ॐ

I WROTE THE FIRST POEM IN MEMORY of my father about five years after his death as a tribute to his molding so many young lives. The other writings are a tribute to Mary Howell's ability to inspire, contain and expand other people's universes.

BLANK SPACE

Blank space is richest
In possibilities unstated
Wisps of unmeasured time
Unmetered affection

Crisp silence
Supporting invisible columns
Of solid caring, nurturing, and blessings.

TENDER GRIEF

Vague strains of music
Reminiscent of Piaf,
Romantic scenes
From lush tropical islands
Somehow,
All of the above,
Bring back images
I'd almost rather forget
Images pulling from the ancients
Secrets from the deepest recesses
Of the perpetual grassy knolls
Images of the forgotten,
The lonely and lost,
Images that seek
To liberate themselves
From their origin,
And to gain entry
To the forbidden gates . . .

I will be true to the promise
To carry on your work,
I will strive to keep on writing,
To keep the voice alive,
That brought me through the darkness
The gentleness with a center of steel,
Now at peace somewhere,
With the memories easing the pain,
The wisdom seeds sprouting
Where the wind scattered them,

With wisps of blessings
Whispering words of encouragement
When the going got rough,
And weather threatens drought . . .

TRIBUTE

From the beginning of time,
All creatures needed a mother,
A source of comfort and nurturing
A haven to grow in safety . . .

My tongue was tied, my voice muted,
My thoughts were formed,
My feelings had no names,
I spoke through my hands and eyes.

I had a speedboat,
With a powerful motor,
Finely tuned for racing,
Grumbling to forge ahead.

You helped me fix my rudder,
Broken off before the journey's start,
Leaving my craft without direction,
At the mercy of hostile winds.

You helped me find my voice,
Lost beyond human reach,
Buried under the oceans' bedrock,
Adrift beyond the cumulus clouds.

You taught me compassion,
Patience and circumspection,
You lived life "to the hilt,"
With conviction and integrity.

Your courage in the face of adversity,
Your tenderness and kindness,
Your support of lost and stumbling souls
Will shine as a beacon for eternity.

WATCHING YOU

I watched you being with your children,
At times smiling and playful
Other times stern and watchful,
Admonishing one and encouraging another,
Praising one and reining back another,
Always balancing, always mindful,
I watched you raise your children.

I watched you tending to your patients, sometimes questioning
Bustling about from office to hospital,
Always caring, sometimes impatient,
Dressing wounds, seeking a deeper healing,
I watched you care for your patients.

I watched you playing music,
Conquering notes, braving intervals,
Smiling with the wind, sailing into vibrato,
Toying with harmony, always listening,
I watched you with your music.

I watched you make peace,
One fragment at a time,
Sliver by sliver,
I watched you make your peace.

SUN AND GRASS

Sun is warm, and grass is green.
If only it were so simple,

But maybe it is,
Just like that recipe,
For pickled fish,
Fry it, and quickly
Steep in soy sauce, wine and sugar.

Sun and grass,
Shall always
Remind me of you,
And that wonderful lawn
With little blue flowers
Welcoming
The broken in spirit
And weary in body.

THE SHADOW OF DEATH

Together again, the shadow of death
Passes over the sky, and hovers
Around our aura, gently holding
All of our old sorrows.

We weep, for today's loss,
And all the prior ones,
The few named losses,
And innumerable silent ones.

Early this morning the moon
Shocked us with its brilliance
Shortly before sunrise,
In the full daylight.

It is the living that carries on
The work of prior generations,
Inspired by the work
Of the ones preceding us.

Some have completed their tasks,
But most leave, a book half-read,
A project in planning stages,
And stories partially told.

It is the living that keeps
The stories going,
The projects flowing
And families bonding.

Time pushes on, inexorably
And we watch, wait and wonder,
Or choose to seize the moment
As it explodes in its own glory.

I search the horizon
For a sign from you,
But you have left
Your imprint on my heart.

I grazed by the piece we played
In York, Maine, almost 25 years ago,
And opted to let its memory lie
Softly in its silent sheath,
Knowing that I shall always hold you
In my hands, and in my heart.

Appendix D

Joe's Poem

Leslie Rizzo's son Joe died unexpectedly a year after graduating law school. Leslie and her husband have three grandchildren—one is named Joey, after his Uncle Joe, and another is named Jessica, after Jessica Zimmerman, who set up a scholarship to honor the memory of her classmate and colleague. Leslie says of her grandchildren, "They are all precious. I know that Joe watches over them every day."

๛

JOE'S POEM

My days are filled with sorrow
The tears flow endlessly
My life is empty and filled with pain
Since the day that you left me

I have no more tomorrows
Only day to day
Things have become so different
It never was this way

I long to hold you, to feel your touch
To hear your voice again
Your laughter always filled the room
Nothing is the same

The things we did together
Simple things to look forward to
I cannot do them anymore
This hurt, I never knew

All these years I've watched you grow
Into an extraordinary man
Only to have you taken away
This cannot be God's plan

What kind of plan, could there be
To cause such hurt and pain
To leave one's life so empty
The loss I can't explain

My heart will always be broken
The pieces I cannot find
To help me put together
My life, my thoughts, my mind

As the years pass, it will get easier
I've heard that's what people say
The pain is constant, never to leave
It will always be that way

I hope one day, I'll see you again
To hold you close to me
To find the love I lost one day
For all ETERNITY

Recipes

In her remembrance, Florie Wachtenheim describes the interest in cooking that she and her mother shared, particularly the dishes that are so much a part of European Jewry's Ashkenazic tradition, in which her mother was raised.

℠

WHEN I WAS GROWING UP, I never imagined that anyone other than my mother made her own gefilte fish. None of my friends' mothers made it, and people were surprised to hear she made her own "from scratch." Gefilte fish was clearly a family favorite on the holidays, both for Rosh Hashanah and for Passover. Because I was certain that my mother held the secret to this recipe, virtually exclusively, it is a recipe that I was sure to have her dictate to me. Her suggestions made an impression—"make sure the water is boiling when you put the fish in" and "don't be skimpy with the sugar and salt." I made the fish a few times while my mother was still alive. It was good, though possibly not quite as good as hers. There was a tremendous sense of accomplishment to be able to make something so "exotic." There was one step I was not prepared to take, that of grinding the fish.

I let her know that I was having the fish merchant grind my fish, something she only accepted as a possibility after she'd seen that it worked out okay (though I don't think she ever let the store grind the fish for her).

My mother's recipe is of the Ashkenazic tradition. Her recipe starts with the inclusion of fish frames and the fish head (all for flavoring of the stock). I promise you that if my mother didn't emphasize its importance, I'd hesitate to include this item. But one new step (like the one from self-ground to store-bought) that I've included—I (double-)wrap these parts in cheesecloth, as opposed to dropping them right into the stock.

I do wonder where my mother got the recipe. She left Poland without many photos, certainly without written recipes. She was twenty years old when she left, so did she already know how to make gefilte fish? Was it a staple that was included for most Sabbath dinners? Did she help her mother prepare it?

Maw Maw's Gefilte Fish (in her words)

Start with 4 lbs. each whitefish and yellow pike. They should be fillets. Ask for the bones and skin and for the head of the carp (with eyes removed). Fish will reduce by half when it is boned and ground.

Into an 8-qt. pot put fish bones, skin and head, a large sliced onion, a small sliced carrot, 4 qts. of water, 1-2 T. salt, 2 T. sugar and some pepper to taste. Bring to an active boil. Lower the flame to medium.

Rinse the fish. Cut a large onion into eighths and slice a carrot. Put all of this into the grinder. (Note: Unlike my mother, I have merchant grind the fish.) Take a hand chopper and use a deep wooden bowl. Put the ground fish mixture into the bowl, add 2 eggs, ½ c. matzoh meal, 1-2 T. salt, some pepper, approximately 2 T. sugar and ½ c. cold water. Chop for about 5 minutes and taste.

Make sure water in pot is boiling!

Put cold water in a dish.

Spoon out the fish mixture onto a wet hand chopper. Flatten the patty onto the chopper.

Add fish patties to the actively boiling water. When all in, adjust the flame to medium. Cook for about 2 hours, covered. Taste the sauce. It shouldn't be watery. [Note: Unlike my mother's, mine always is.] When cool, remove the fish. Strain the sauce. Remove the bones. (Mine are in cheesecloth.) Refrigerate.

[Note: My mother got the stock to gel. She liked to serve the fish with the gel. I have never been able to get mine to gel . . . and probably never will!]

Next on to the rugelach, affectionately termed "ruggies." My mother made these for as long as I can remember, but changed to this recipe (which a friend gave her) at some point. Our family enjoyed this recipe very much.

Ann's food grinder.

Rugelach

3 c. sifted flour
1 package dry yeast
½ lb. butter (or ¼ lb. butter, ¼ lb. margarine), at room temperature
3 egg yolks
1 c. sugar
1 c. chopped nuts
1 ½ t. cinnamon
Strawberry, raspberry or apricot preserves (optional)

Sprinkle yeast over flower. Cut in shortening until crumbly. Stir egg yolks into sour cream and add to flour mixture. Chill this dough overnight.

Divide chilled dough into 4 parts.

Mix sugar, nuts and cinnamon together. Sprinkle ¼ of this mixture onto a board and spread it into a circle. Take one of your 4 parts of dough, put it on top of the sugar/nuts/cinnamon mixture, and roll it out into a circle. Spread some preserves around the outer rim of the circle. Cut the circle into 16ths. Roll pastry up from the outside in. Repeat this process 4 times.

Place on greased cookie sheets and bake at 325 degrees for 25 minutes.

Freezes well.

Afterword

by Meryl Ain

THIS BOOK BEGAN AS AN EXPLORATION of how to pay tribute to our mother in a meaningful way, but we also wanted to memorialize our father, who died at eighty-eight—nineteen months before she did. We also hoped to assist others in helping to perpetuate the memories of their loved ones. The deaths of our parents were very different. While our mother was attacked by an aggressive cancer and taken from us within a matter of months, our father was ill for ten years, his health deteriorating incrementally over time from a variety of causes. After she was gone, it was easy to conjure up memories of our mother, because she remained essentially the same until the week she died. Remembering our father in his prime would require more effort.

As we were researching and writing the book, the answer became apparent. It came from our interviewees, most notably Nick Clooney and Yeou-Cheng Ma, who suggested that one of the most accessible ways of honoring a loved one was to establish a scholarship in his or her memory.

It was not long until the light bulb went on in my head. As a teacher and principal in the Brentwood (Long Island) Public Schools, my father had a successful and meaningful career there for twenty-five years. Tempered by the crucible of World War II, where he served in the U.S. Army in Europe, and with a career in business behind him, he entered public education after his fortieth birthday, determined to make a difference.

So I established the Herbert J. Fischman Memorial Scholarship and agreed to grant two five-hundred-dollar scholarships the first year—one to a girl and one to a boy. I was invited to present these scholarships at the Brentwood High School Annual Awards Assembly in May. There I joined with many others to award hundreds of scholarships to Brentwood's deserving graduates. Many of the students are awarded multiple scholarships, so while most of the individual scholarships are modest, they can add up, and numerous students receive sizeable support.

While the students were the recipients of the scholarships, attending the assembly and presenting the scholarships was both cathartic and therapeutic for me. In addition, listening to others speak about their loved ones confirmed that dedicating a scholarship, no matter what the amount, helps to keep alive the memory of those who are no longer here.

An added bonus was meeting two retired teachers who worked in my father's school, and who shared with me their reminiscences, as well as their affection and admiration for my dad. My father became more fully alive for me that evening than he had been in more than fifteen years. Both of the young people followed up with thank-you letters, which confirmed the feeling. Here are some excerpts:

"It is with great appreciation that I thank you and your family for allowing me to be one of the recipients of the $500 Herbert J. Fischman Memorial Scholarship. Words can't describe how grateful my family and I are for your help towards my future. In this economy every little bit helps.

"I would like to thank you for your generosity and support toward my college education. I would also like to pay respect to your father since he did serve in the community for an outstanding 25 years and is most likely respected by former colleagues and students. It still must be tough to cope with this loss since it is just over five years, but I know he still lives through people like you who give back to the community of Brentwood.

"I am of Mexican and Haitian descent and I will be the first in my family to attend college. I am blessed that I am one of the recipients of your scholarship. I will work hard to keep the spirit of your father alive and I will not let you down."

To our readers: If you have a story to share about how you have kept alive the spirit, values or personality of a departed loved one, through either an idea of your own or one inspired by a story in this book, please send it to LivingMemoriesProject@gmail.com. We are currently compiling narratives for the second volume of *The Living Memories Project*.

And, be sure to visit our website at thelivingmemoriesproject.com.

Best wishes,

Meryl Ain, Ed. D.
Arthur M. Fischman
Stewart Ain

"God gave us memory that we might have roses in December."
— James M. Barrie —

Index

About the Authors

MERYL AIN holds a BA from Queens College, an MA from Columbia University Teachers College, and an Ed.D. from Hofstra University. She began her career in education as a social studies teacher before she became an administrator. She is also a freelance writer specializing in issues related to education, families, parenting, and children and has contributed to *Huffington Post*, *Newsday*, the *New York Jewish Week* and the *New York Times*. She embarked on *The Living Memories Project* after she lost both her father and mother within a year and a half. She and her husband, Stewart, live on Long Island and have three sons, three daughters-in-law, and three grandchildren.

Meryl Ain

ಐ

ARTHUR M. FISCHMAN holds a BA from Queens College and a JD from Temple Law School. He is a freelance writer whose video and interactive scripts have won numerous awards, including a Telly, an ITVA Silver Award, and a New York Festivals Bronze World Medal. He co-wrote the award-winning documentary *Digital Dharma* and has written radio, TV, and print ads for leading consumer product manufacturers. Arthur is a veteran speechwriter and ghostwriter, and was director of execu-tive communications and internal com-

Arthur M. Fischman

munications for a Fortune 500 company. He, his wife, and their two daughters live in Philadelphia, where he also writes plays and moon-lights as a jazz pianist.

ಶಿ

STEWART AIN is a graduate of CW Post College and holds an MA from the Columbia University Graduate School of Journalism. He is an award-winning journalist with more than forty years of experience, and was a Pulitzer Prize nominee three times. He has reported for the *New York Times*, *New York Daily News*, *New York Jewish Week*, *Long Island Business News*, and *Lifestyles Maga-zine*. Stewart frequently appears on tele-vision and radio, and hosts his own weekly cable TV program, *Jewish Life*, and has been a regular guest on *The Leon*

Stewart Ain

Charney Show. Both his parents died while he was working on *The Living Memories Project*.